MY CAT SAMMY

My Cat Sammy

ETHEL MANNIN

Photographs by F. W. Ziemsen

London
MICHAEL JOSEPH

First published in Great Britain by
MICHAEL JOSEPH LTD
52 Bedford Square
London W.C.1
1971

7181 0885 X

Set and printed in Great Britain by
Tonbridge Printers Ltd, Peach Hall Works, Tonbridge, Kent
in Bembo twelve on fourteen point on paper supplied by
P. F. Bingham Ltd, and bound by James Burn
at Esher, Surrey

To

'TIM'

*who knows both the author
and the cat, and who took
the pictures. . . .*

The author is grateful to M. B. Yeats and Macmillan & Co. for permission to quote four lines from the poem *The Cat and the Moon* from *The Collected Poems of W. B. Yeats*.

ILLUSTRATIONS

Chapter One

EVEN as a child I had a 'thing' about cats. It was not just the child's natural love for animals, for I seem to have been singularly lacking in that – I had no particular feeling for puppies, was downright afraid of dogs, and never wanted a pet rabbit, but cats aroused a kind of love in me. I think it was love. It seemed to come welling up from deep down inside me, almost anguished. Especially if a cat was what my mother called a 'stray'. I never had a cat as a child; my father disliked them and would have liked a dog; my mother didn't care much for dogs and was fond of cats, but was very house-proud and fussy and declared you were better without *any* animals; it was different, she said vaguely, in the country. Certainly there were cats galore on my grandfather's farm, my mother's home, but they were outside cats and not allowed in the house. They were given saucers of skimmed milk after milking time, but had otherwise to fend for themselves; there were after all plenty of mice in the barn. Occasionally they got a few scraps when we children were there, and I worried about them, wondering if they got enough to eat. It seems I started worrying about cats early on. About the strays who occasionally came around where we lived in south London I worried a great deal. My mother would always give a stray a saucer of milk, and stroke the 'poor thing', as she called it, but she would never take it in; if it was still sitting hopefully on the doorstep after dark she would pick it up and carry it to another street, some way off, and when she came to what seemed a suitable house she would put it down in the front garden and hurry away. A suitable house was one in which there was a light in the window, showing that the people were at home, and where there were neat curtains at the windows, showing that respectable people lived there – you could always tell by the curtains, my mother would declare; she was right, too. The assumption was that decent people, respectable people, would always take in a stray cat. We had very neat curtains at our windows – my mother took a pride in them, cream lace they were, and always very clean – and my mother was very decent and respectable, and liked cats into the bargain, but she never took one in. But as a child I accepted it that a stray cat deposited outside a lighted window, with good curtains, would be all right. Only sometimes when we were out on walks, or shopping, I would see a thin-looking cat I would feel sure was a stray, and then I worried. I never owned a cat until I was grown-up and married and had a child of my own.

We seemed, then, to have a succession of cats, but they were more my daughter's cats than mine. There was one she brought home from boarding-school at the end of term; it was 'special' because it had been born up a tree, but in spite of the unique circumstances of its birth no one wanted it, and the lady-who-ran-the-school said it would have to be 'put to sleep'. It ended up with my mother, of all people; she took it as much as anything because by then I had a little sister – which was very unfair when you came to think of my own catless childhood. Anyhow she took it and it lived with her to a great age, but it was never allowed beyond the kitchen; my mother remained house-proud and fussy to the end of her long life. My father resolutely ignored the cat. Once in my presence he opened a tin of sardines for it, my mother being away, and set the saucer down on newspaper in a corner of the kitchen with the harsh words, 'There you are, you blinkin' parasite!'

The cat only briefly outlived my father, and my poor mother was doubly bereaved. My father was cremated, and the cat given earth burial in the garden.

There was a cat, too – for some reason we called him Tipsy – who unaccountably left the comfortable home he had with us – in a detached house standing in a large garden – and went off to live in a terrace house in a rather drab street. My daughter and I came upon him sitting on the window sill. He allowed us to stroke him but gave no sign of recognition. We knocked on the door and to the woman of the house we said politely, 'We think you have our cat!' She exclaimed, 'Oh, is he yours? We wondered where he came from.' Then added, anxiously, 'I do hope you don't want him back? The children are so fond of him.'

Since he had not batted a whisker over our finding him, we left Tipsy there, and he watched us go with complete indifference.

I asked my daughter, then in her teens, as we walked away, 'Why do you suppose he left us to go and live there?'

'Perhaps,' she said, 'he went in search of his crown jewels – which we took away.'

In the thirties there was a very beautiful thoroughbred cat, a cream Persian, given me by a fan. I called him Tomaselli, after my favourite café in Salzburg, but for some reason I never had much affection for him. He wasn't really my idea of a *cat*. What I have always liked about cats is their *catness*.

This beautiful hairy little animal for me lacked that essential quality. My housekeeper – we had that kind of domestic help in those days – adored him, and was heartbroken when, like Lycidas, he died ere his prime. I was living in Paris a good deal at that time, and receiving the news in Montparnesse was strangely unmoved. He had never really been 'my' cat. Perhaps I was prejudiced against him from the start, because he was thoroughbred, and given me by an upper-class fan, and I like common or garden cats, and common or garden people. He was a pretty, delicate thing, but a cat should be feline, tough, sinuous. Is he not, after all, related to the 'noblest cat of all', the tiger? The cat this book is really about is such a cat; he is the colour of a tiger, has the wonderful markings of a tiger, is tough and feline and *cat*.

But before him there was Lucy, the devil-cat, who lived with me for sixteen years, beautiful and indifferent, producing kittens galore, black kittens and tabby kittens and mixed kittens, and finally a monster kitten . . . after which, unable to cope any longer with the full-time job she made of her sex life, I had her spayed. Against my principles, but sometimes principle is the handmaid of expediency, and the vet gave me absolution by declaring that it was 'either a spayed cat or a dead cat', for the next pregnancy, he said, would be extra-uterine. Well, perhaps. He should know. Anyhow, I had her spayed.

Lucy was under sentence of death when I took her as a kitten in 1950. She seemed too young and beautiful to die. She, also, was not really my idea of a cat, being long-haired and black. She was *cat*, though, half-wild, neither giving nor seeking affection, a great hunter in her day, and driven in season by overpowering lust. She could leap like a tiger, too; almost to the end of her life she was capable of that great spring, from a flower-bed about six feet up to a low roof; it was fascinating to watch her 'gathering' herself for it, like a horse at a high jump. From the low roof she would go on up over a steep tiled gable to a window; in my absences she would make for the window of a small room in which food would have been left down for her, and which she inhabited; when I was here she would go unerringly to whichever room, study or bedroom, I was occupying. I do not know how she knew in which room I was, and when I was not there, whether it was her cat's fantastic sense of smell, or equally fantastic hearing, but know she did.

With her total lack of demonstrativeness, seldom purring, never getting into a lap, she was an unrewarding cat – except that the beauty and grace of a cat, any cat, is a reward in itself. A cat is, quite simply, a beautiful creature to have around – vastly more beautiful than the majority of human beings. If it throws in affection as well that is a bonus. Lucy was the devil-cat because as a kitten she would dart about, always in mischief, like a little black devil, and because when she was older by her sheer impersonalness she conveyed something satanic – there was some *je ne sais quoi* in those slitty green eyes. She was called Lucy because, being female, she could not be called Lucifer.

In the last year or so of her life she failed a lot, as cats do towards the end. She became very thin, and had trouble with her teeth. Cats collect tartar on their teeth, and it has to be removed or they cannot eat properly. I had the vet to her once for this purpose. Two nights before she died she seemed in a bad way, and I telephoned the vet and he said he would send for her in the morning – it would be best, he thought, if he had her up there and gave her a good going-over. From that point on I made, I now think, a series of mistakes; I record them for the guidance of other cat-owners as well-meaning and wrong as I was. The first mistake was in thinking that a cat as old as that could benefit by dental attention. That night she wanted to go out, but it was a freezing night and I thought that, so frail and thin as she was, she should stay in the warmth of the kitchen; that was my second mistake; I should have let her go; a cat knows its own business best; her animal need was to go out into the night for the last time to die, as nature intended, in the open; but I kept her in.

In the morning I let her out, and she made her way slowly to the end of the garden, as far away as possible from the house, to lie beside a pond, from which she occasionally drank. I knew then that she was dying, and I telephoned the vet. He was not available, but I spoke to a nurse. I said I was afraid this cat was on the way out since I rang last night, and there was no point now in having her collected for attention to her teeth. The nurse said, oh, but a lot could be done for an old cat, 'with injections', whatever that might have meant, and their van was already on the way to collect her. I should have insisted that I didn't want her collected, but I allowed myself to be over-ruled by what I believed was superior knowledge. When the van arrived she was lying at the foot of a yew tree, the sun having reached that point by then. She could have died peacefully there in that patch of sunlight, but driven by good intentions I went out and picked her up and carried her back into the house; when we reached the door she made a small whimper of protest, but resolutely, steeling myself to it, I carried her into the house and put her into the basket the man from the vet's had brought, and by which he stood, waiting for her.

I put her in and he strapped down the lid. He remarked as he picked up the basket how light she was. He inquired how old she was; sixteen, I told him. He remarked, cheerfully, that not many cats reached that age nowadays, they were mostly run over by cars . . .

She did not whimper as he carried the basket down the garden path to the van. I felt miserable; I felt so damn miserable I could have cried, and inside myself I did. I went shopping, and I bought a jar of chicken essence to give her, as a treat, when she was brought back that evening. Around lunchtime, when I was back from the shopping, the vet rang; he had seen to her teeth, he said, but there was more than that wrong with her; it was her kidneys, he thought; he would like to keep her overnight; to make a urine test, he said. That was my last mistake; I said all right, to keep her.

The following morning he rang to say she had 'died in her sleep'. He meant, of course, that she had just plain died. It was a pity she had to die there, in a cage, at the vet's, instead of here in the familiar surroundings. In the end I had betrayed her; pushed her into a basket; let her be taken away. But letting her go, that wasn't my last mistake; the last mistake was not having her brought back here. I should have had her brought back and buried her in the garden and planted a rose bush over her, for her small corpse to nourish. Only at the time I couldn't think straight. I had made so many mistakes. And I was so damn miserable.

Yet her death led to the advent here of the strong young life of the shining golden tiger-cat, Sammy, the *little* feller . . .

Chapter Two

IN retrospect I suppose that if I had not sent Lucy to the vet that bright cold September morning, but allowed her to die here in the garden as she had wanted, I should have tormented myself with the thought that 'if only I'd sent her to the vet he might have been able to do something for her! I should have given her the chance.' I think I would have thought that, at a distance of four years from the event, I am quite sure I made a mistake that morning; that she had no chance, that an animal knows when its time has come, and that a cat, of all creatures has the right to die in the open, in the place of its choice, and that humans oppose Nature when they attempt to intervene.

I thought a great deal about the whole subject of intervention after Lucy's death. I thought so much about it that the following year I wrote a novel* round the idea of the dangerousness of intervening in anyone's life – if one had not introduced So-and-So to So-and-So this or that unhappiness or tragedy would never have happened; we take such risks with other people's happiness by our interventions in their lives – our meddlesome good intentions. Our intervention in the lives of animals is monstrous. We have power of life and death over them. We intervene, for our own convenience, and take their sex from them; or we intervene as to when they shall mate, and what shall be done with their offspring; we intervene to decide, very often, when

* *Bitter Babylon*, 1968.

they shall die, and how, and where. There is the credit side, to be sure; I intervened in Lucy's life early on and saved her from being put to death; as a result she had a long, and I think happy, life; to save something beautiful from destruction, that surely is good. Intervention is not always bad; it can sometimes be good; but it is always risky. The Buddhists are right, I think, in their philosophy of non-intervention, leaving all things living to work out their own *karma*, unhindered, free of interference. I once met a Buddhist in Burma who argued that logically one should not give, for example, to a beggar likely to die of hunger, for to do so might prolong his life in this incarnation, in which his lot was obviously bad, whereas by not intervening he might be released the sooner into a happier existence. Given belief in the inexorable laws of *karma* and rebirth the argument is indisputably logical.

But though at the time of Lucy's death I vowed I would never again intervene in the life of an animal or a human being, I nevertheless intervened again in the life of a cat a few months later when, to some friends about to emigrate, and exercised as to what to do about their cat, I uttered the fatal words, 'If nobody else wants him I'd love to have him! . . . ' Fatal words because, of course, after that they made no further efforts to find him a home. If I had not intervened in this way he would have gone, in all probability, to a neighbour who did not much care for cats but who would have taken him, reluctantly, under pressure from the children. He would have had a rough sort of life in a rough sort of district, but it would have been terrain he knew, with plenty of unspayed females around – which in this middle-class residential area, where almost everyone has a dog, there are not. The food wouldn't have been as good, and the home-comforts non-existent, but as an entire male cat he would have had a rich and full life, and whilst an undoctored cat accepts the human mod cons when they are available, it doesn't need them; they're not important; sex and freedom are.

A French vet, Dr Fernand Méry, gives a very good example of this in his wonderful book, *The Life, History and Magic of the Cat.** He tells of a cat called Alfonso, a Paris cat, 'who knew Colette and was indeed at home to all Paris.' He had the good fortune to be brought to live at a restaurant, where the quality of the food and shelter were very good, but because he was a *cat*, an entire cat, and therefore *nocturnal*, Alfonso went out every night, in wind and rain and snow, and stayed out. His owner told Dr Méry that often on cold wet nights he had tried to force him to remain indoors in the warmth, but in the end he was obliged to agree that Alfonso knew his own business best, and that gourmet though he was, and affectionate though he was, first and foremost he was a 'wanderer in the night'.

Dr Méry comments, out of forty years experience of observing feline behaviour, 'There exist for the cat truths which have nothing in common with human truths. The cat does not question us in order to form its own opinion about us. It does not, like the dog, seek to read in our eyes what is good and what is bad. It is not ignorant of the fact that some things are forbidden, but its knowledge is that of someone outside the law, for whom justice is not the judge but the gamekeeper.'

Someone outside the law. The essentially wild creature. *The cat that walked alone, in the wild wet woods.* When, no doubt, it could have been sitting cosily by the domestic hearth.

* English edition, 1968. Trans. from *Le Chat*, 1966, by Emma Street.

But it is first and foremost a wanderer in the night. Why do humans so often try to debase this free splendid spirit with their pretty-pussy sentimentalities? Colette, who really knew about cats, had too great a respect for them even to give them names; they were simply Cat; *le chat*. Nevertheless cats do know their names, if they are given them in kittenhood. Lucy knew her name and would come when called; her mother, Mitzi, my daughter's cat, knew her name; if it was even mentioned in conversation she would immediately look up. But this adopted cat does not know his name; officially it is Sami, from the Arabic, corrupted into English as Sammy; I called him Sami after the little boy, Samir, whose cat he specially was; before that if he was called anything it was Ginger – which is no name for a handsome little tiger; in moments of exasperation I address him as Cat. 'Oh, Cat,' I say, 'what a little nuisance you are!' In the evenings, when after a thorough wash-and-brush-up he indicates that he is ready to go out, I say, 'All right then, Cat, come along!' and he comes along. Usually, before he goes off out into the night, he has a fit of rolling about, as though inviting admiration, and, indeed, the more he is assured that he is the *most* beautiful pussy-cat the more he rolls, front legs lifted, displaying his lovely honey-coloured belly. Then, suddenly, he springs to his feet, like a man who really has fooled around long enough and is now rather pressed for time, and it is my cue to see him off out into the night, which I do, wet or fine, come-hell-or-high-water. Indeed, there was a midnight in mid-winter when I went out into the garden and swept some paths for him through the snow, and he skipped about like a young lamb around my broom. There was a brightness like moonlight from the snow; it was still and beautiful; but freezing hard, and when I had swept a path the length of a long border, and a track up through the rhododendrons to the tall elms at the top of the slope, I had had enough and went back to the house. At the door, with the lighted room behind me, I called to him, 'Coming in now, Pussy-cat? *Cold* out there!' He looked at me across the snow, some yards distant on the swept path, and his look said plainly, 'Coming *in*? Whatever for?' I went in, filled a hot water bottle, made a hot drink, and went snugly to bed. Settling under the blankets with a book I thought of him out there in the white freezing night; but it was the way he wanted it; he had, I reflected, his high animal blood temperature, and his fine thick fur coat, grown specially for the winter – for such nights as this.

In the morning when I went down and opened the dining-room door on to the covered loggia he was curled up on his blanket in an old armchair. He did not move but opened an eye.

'Hello, Cat,' I said, 'coming in for breakfast?'

He closed the eye and buried his head deeper into his front paws. Snubbed, I went back to bed myself, but with *The Times*, tea, and toast.

Lucy slept in at nights, not because she wanted to, for mostly she didn't, but because I – mistakenly – insisted. But she had that same cat disregard for the human values. She would be lying stretched out in front of the fire, luxuriating in the warmth, then would suddenly sit up, tidy up a little, stalk across the room and demand to go out; outside she would sit on cold wet paving stones, or on frozen snow, or wet grass. As Gertrude Stein might have said, a cat is a cat is a cat. That is what is so splendid about cats. They are unpredictable; *different*.

Chapter Three

So, by way of the death of Lucy, the devil-cat, we come to Sami, the tiger-cat, commonly known as Sammy.

We did not meet for the first time that day I went to lunch to say goodbye to the emigrating friends: we had in fact met three years earlier when I was at the house, and the youngest of the three children, the boy called Samir, was wandering about clutching a small ginger kitten. He had found it, his mother said, on his way home from school, and he wanted to keep it; she didn't mind, but her husband was against it. The husband declared, firmly, 'We don't want a *cat*!'

'We do!' young Samir insisted, stormily. '*I* want a cat!'

'It's not what *you* want,' his father said.

The boy's eyes filled with rebellious tears and he rushed out, the kitten half choked in his impassioned grip.

I pleaded, 'It seems a pity not to let him have it, as he found it. He desperately wants it.'

'He can't have everything he wants,' the father said.

His wife said nothing. I had the feeling she would have the last word.

I murmured to her, when I left, 'I do hope Samir is allowed to keep the kitten.'

She said, simply, 'We'll keep it.'

How was I to know I was booking myself a little tiger-cat – to be delivered to me in a few years' time? When I walked into that same sitting-room three years later and exclaimed, 'Oh, what a lovely cat!' I had long forgotten the ginger kitten. This cat, anyhow, was nothing so common as ginger; he was a delicious honey colour; only on his back were there dark tawny stripes. Tiger stripes. A tiger is not 'ginger'.

My hostess said, reproachfully, 'You remember Samir's kitten? It was you who said we should keep him.' She added, as though it were all my fault, 'Now, of course, we don't know what to do with him . . .'

'Surely,' I urged, 'it can't be difficult to find a home for a handsome cat like that – a *male* cat?'

'Everyone round here has a cat already!'

It was then I heard myself uttering the fatal words, 'If no one else wants him I'd *love* to have him!'

Uttered against all my convictions that a-cat-is-a-tie, a-nuisance-when-you-want-to-go-away, and, as my mother said more than half a century ago, you're-better-off-without-*any*-animals. But when you have this thing about cats, what wells up in your heart comes out of your mouth in words that commit you against your better judgment.

'*I'd love to have him.*'

And so, of course, I got him.

I'd said he must be taken first to the vet's to be neutered; I'd thought it would help him to settle down in his new environment if he had no impulse to wander; I had also thought he would stand no chance of a sex life in this 'dog' area.

In due course he was brought all across London from Ilford to Wimbledon, via the tube during the rush-hour, God help all concerned, and left at the designated vet's. A few days later I was notified by telephone that he had 'had his operation' and was 'ready to come home'.

I said to keep him another day as I was going to the theatre that night and would naturally want to be here with him his first night here. He was brought next morning. In the same big basket in which they had taken Lucy away. I am sure it was the same basket. A big, ugly, horrible basket. He was yelling his head off when the man in the overall who had taken Lucy away carried him up the front garden path. I have never heard a cat yell so loudly, and hope I never will again. It was a cry for help, help, HELP!

The big ugly basket was brought into the kitchen and the man in the brown overall let him out. He sprang out, yelling, yelling. He was frantic. I said to the man, helplessly, 'Leave him to me. I'll manage him.'

The man went away with his basket, his beastly basket, and the little tiger and I were left alone together. He ran wildly behind the kitchen boiler, yelling, yelling, help, help, HELP. I was pretty frantic myself. I also wanted help. I brought out of the larder the chicken's liver I'd got him – I'd asked the vet not to feed him before he was brought to me. I crouched on the floor with the saucer of chicken's liver, and I called to him, softly, 'Pussy-cat. Pussy-cat.' He came out from behind the boiler and when he saw the saucer ran to it and began to eat, hungrily. I stroked him and spoke softly to him – 'It's all right, pussy-cat. It's all right.' When he had eaten I carried him upstairs to the study, stroking him, speaking softly to him. We sat down on the floor in front of the fire together, but he stayed only a moment, then wandered around, yelling loudly, trying to find a way out. He ended up on a bookshelf by the door. I stroked him, talked to him, carried him to the divan. On and off he purred a little, then panic would overcome him, and it would begin again, help! help! HELP! Then he went into

23

a corner and urinated, and there was a powerful tomcat smell. Odd, I thought, in a neutered cat. Then I remembered what the vet had said – that for a time he would 'still have some hormones to dispose of'.

After that he settled down for a while on the divan and slept, as though exhausted – and perhaps he was – by the upset of it all. When he woke he began yelling and prowling again. I opened the door thinking he should perhaps acquaint himself with the geography of the house. He went into the bedroom and had diarrhoea in a corner. His former owner had told me that he was a 'very clean' cat, and cats, in general, *are* very clean. But this was obviously a very upset cat.

I cleaned up the mess, then took him out into the garden and carried him around, so that he would know the geography of the garden too. Presently I put him down, and he made off into the rhododendrons. I plunged in after him and brought him out, and he struggled and protested. I brought him back into the house, into the study, and then it started all over again, the prowling and the yelling – help, help, HELP!

At the end of five hours I could stand it no longer. I carried him downstairs and put him out in the garden. I stood at the door of the dining-room and watched him heading off up the slope towards the boundary fence behind the tall elms; heading off into the unknown. It was terrible. Would he make a bid to get back to his old home, at the other side of London? Would his cat's sixth sense, the sense of direction, stand up to the confusion of all that tube travel and the days at the vet's? And once he had left this garden how far would he get, with the traffic hurtling along the main road?

I was quite sure I would never see him again, the little feller.

Despairingly I telephoned Tim, an old friend who had loved Lucy and who had been much interested in the acquisition of this new cat. When he answered the telephone he said at once, eagerly, 'You've got the cat?'

I told him, forlornly, 'I had him – for five hours.'

'What happened?' Alarm in his voice.

I told him.

He exclaimed, incredulously, 'You let him *go*?'

'I had to!' I cried. 'I couldn't stand it any longer. You'd have done the same! It was driving me crazy . . .'

It didn't help that he said, distressed, that it was terrible.

'Leave food down,' he urged. 'He might come back. You never know. Hunger might send him back.'

I left food down when I went to bed at midnight. It was still there in the morning. And every morning that week.

Tim came at the week-end and we scoured the garden together – a large garden, on different levels, and full of hideouts. In the jungly part at the top of the slope Tim, searching alone, found some honey-coloured hair. He brought it to me in the house.

'Is this the colour of the cat?'

I said it was, and asked where he had found it. He said in a hollowed-out nest of dry leaves amongst all the elm-suckers and undergrowth. So he was still around – that was something. He must be very hungry by now, unless he was managing to catch field mice such as Lucy used to bring in from the garden, alive, so that my late husband used to say, bitterly, 'People have cats to keep mice away – ours brings them in!'

25

The second week the food put down overnight was gone in the morning, every morning, but I could not be sure whether the right cat had had it, for I began to observe other cats around. The following Sunday Tim once again scouring the garden came excitedly into the house.

'I'm sure he's here,' he cried. 'Under the bushes by the pergola. A big yellow cat – the colour of honey – '

I went out and he was there, right enough, the little feller, crouching amongst the dead leaves, under the shrubs beside the pergola. I peered in and spoke to him, and he hissed. I went back into the house and put pet-food into a saucer and took it out to the shrubbery and pushed it into him. He ate, ravenously, but when I put in a hand to stroke him, to reassure him, as I thought, he hissed.

Well, anyhow, it was a start. I was sure he would not go away now. Later I saw him making his way along under a low wall, and was dismayed to see that he limped badly, and he looked very thin. He saw me, but ignored me and went on up to the rhododendrons.

Tim suggested, 'Don't give him any more food in the bushes – make him come down to the house for it; leave it on the loggia.'

'How will I know he gets it? There are other cats around.'

'Leave the door open. Try and watch for him.'

'This freezing weather?' I asked, bitterly.

He shrugged.

'You want this cat. You'll have to work to get it.'

Echoes of India, and my Indian forestry-officer host declaring, as we bulldozed our way through the jungles on elephant back, he and my daughter and I, hearing the tiger call but the great cat always eluding us, 'You have to work very hard for your tiger!'

I worked very hard for that very little tiger, the honey-coloured cat. For weeks, evening after evening, I would crouch by the electric fire in the dining-room, the door open on to the loggia, the incoming coldness all but quenching the small glow of heat from the fire; every evening at dusk; just as in the Indian jungles we had gone out every evening at sundown, when, as the Indians said, it was no longer possible to see the lines on your hand; we would go down then to the elephant lines, when the jungle was coming alive with the sounds of the night, the calls of night-birds, and sometimes the blood-chilling call of the tiger, *Ah-humm*! *Ah-humm*! I, the tiger!

It would all come back to me, crouching there, listening to the call of owls and nightjars in this garden, waiting for this very little tiger. When he came – and he always did come – it would be almost too dark to make out his colouring, and one evening the cat that came was not the right one. I recharged the saucers with pet food and milk and the right one came later, no longer furtive but marching boldly up to the saucers which I had placed just inside the door on to the loggia. The long refectory table was between us, I crouching beside the fire, he over the saucer by the door. 'Pussy-cat,' I said softly, coaxingly, but he went on eating, ignoring the overture. 'Pussy-cat,' I entreated, but he did not look up.

When he had eaten he lapped from the saucer of milk, taking his time, finishing it. Then he straightened up, gave himself a little shake, and as deliberately and unhurriedly as he had arrived, marched out into the night. I got up and went to the door and watched him cross the loggia, mount the steps to the paved path above, and disappear into the dusk. He did not look back.

My feelings as I closed the door on to the loggia, switched off the fire, carried the emptied saucers through to the kitchen, were mixed. There was the feeling of satisfaction that the little feller had had a good meal, that he knew now where the good meals were, and had actually set foot in the house; that he had come fearlessly, confidently, seen me and accepted me. All that was to the good. But there was also the bleak feeling that all I was doing was feeding a cat; as it might have been any stray cat – except, I thought bitterly, that a stray cat would have been only too glad to attach itself to me.

But after that I, too, became bolder. He came regularly, around half-past five, but I put the saucers further and further into the dining-room – cautiously at first, only a little, then more boldly, from half way across the room right to the door into the hall. He marched in, unafraid, confidently, ate and drank, then marched out again – like a man who goes every evening to the local, downs his pint, nods to the bar-tender, and goes. Except that this chap went without even a nod to the bar-tender; not even a glance.

When I had got him as far as the door into the hall I would sit on the stairs, waiting and watching. In a house without central heating this was a very cold operation in January, though not as cold as crouching in the dining-room with the door open to the garden. He would stalk across the room to the tray with the two saucers on it, and he would see me sitting on the stairs, but take no notice; he would eat and drink, taking his time, and go. The evening I descended the stairs and approached him he ever so slightly quickened his pace, and by the time I had reached the loggia door had disappeared into the night.

The next evening I placed the tray at the foot of the stairs and seated myself only a few steps away. He looked up before settling to his meal.

'Hullo, Pussycat,' I said.

He merely lowered his head and began to eat. I ventured a few stairs lower and reached out a hand and touched the big honey-coloured head; he looked up, hissed, and went on eating. I made no further advances that evening; it was something, anyhow, that he had not left when I touched him.

The next evening when he arrived I was not sitting on the stairs but on the rug in the hall, and only the small tray with the saucers on it separated us. He looked at me then got down to his supper. When he had finished I touched his head, lightly; he looked up, hissed, and left, stalking away, firmly, unhurriedly, only very slightly quickening his step as I approached.

It was progress of a kind, I supposed; at least he was eating in the house.

It went on like this, evening after evening, week after week. Before he arrived I would resolve that that evening I was going to stroke him, whether he liked it or not, whether he hissed or spat or both. But when he came I dared not; I was so desperately afraid of offending him. One evening, though, I did stroke his head; he did not hiss, but also he did not stay.

There was an evening when he did not come. No less than four cats came in the hours in which I waited, but not the honey-coloured cat; they did not come into the hall; finding no food at the loggia door they circled around a bit then melted away into the night. Somewhere around midnight I closed the door into the garden, and I did not leave food out. I was very puzzled about that procession of

29

cats, for I had seen no cats about since Lucy died. After the advent of Sammy-cat there had been cats around again – a big old tabby cat, a real battered old tom, and a young, dark tomcat; and there had been some spraying. Why should they come? Had the smell of a new cat in the district been borne on the wind? Had the news gone around that there was a new cat in town? But why the spraying? The new cat was not a female. Could it be that hope springs eternal in the tomcat breast? Or that the cats of the neighbourhood came out of curiosity to see the newcomer? In the past, except when Lucy was in season, I seldom saw another cat, this not being a cat district. When Lucy was in season cats turned up in a marvellous assortment, the good news of a queen in season having gone down the wind, borne far and wide. Even after she was spayed they would turn up in the 'cat months', March and November, her old lovers, to whom she would never again be of any use, and I would feel guilty. But for this young eunuch, new to the district, why should they come? Did they mistake him for a female? If they did they were soon disillusioned, for Sammy had made this garden his territory and he refused to tolerate intruders . . . which is strictly in accord with tiger policy. The tiger has his own beat of about three miles, and if any male tiger strays into it so much the worse for him. Sammy had obviously been involved in a fight the day he first emerged from the bushes and went limping along the wall; now he was continuously involved in fights; there would be scuffles and caterwaulings after dark, and Sammy would return from these affrays a wounded warrior, limping, even going on three legs at times, and with head scratches. Someone knowledgeable about cats told me that a cat new to a district had a hard time of it for some weeks defending his territory. I could accept this, but that a neutered cat should lead so normal a tomcat life, defending territory and becoming involved in fights – that puzzled me.

But once it began it went on – the visiting cats, with the battered old tom the most persistent, and he in turn involved in fights with the young tom, the affrays, the hissing and snarling, the scuffles, but Sammy still turning up on time for the evening meal, usually hissing if I touched him, and always walking away when he had supped. Sometimes it seemed as though I had progressed as far as I was ever going to; all January went by, and half of February, and I was still no more than feeding this honey-coloured cat; there was a sense in which he had adopted me, as his provider, but my plans for adopting him were not working out.

One cold sunny February afternoon I looked out of my study window and saw him sitting on the slope, in front of the rhododendrons. He was sitting bolt upright and looking at the house. A clump of the first snowdrops were in bloom beside him. It was a charming picture. I opened the window and spoke softly.

'Hullo, pussy-cat!'

He looked at me – and the Matthew Arnold lines came to me:

> *'Cruel, but composed and bland,*
> *Dumb, inscrutable and grand,*
> *So Tiberius might have sat,*
> *Had Tiberius been a cat.'*

Cruel? Well, perhaps. But hardly more so than Man. Inscrutable certainly. I closed the window and went downstairs and out on to the loggia. I went up the steps and stood

31

at the bottom of the slope and we regarded each other, only a few yards apart.

'Pussy-cat,' I beseeched, and held out a hand.

He rose, turned his back, and disappeared into the rhododendrons, and I returned to the house. The time, evidently, was not yet; but he had emerged in broad daylight; he had sat in contemplation of the house, as though weighing up the pros and cons of moving in, taking up residence. I think that in his cat-fashion he was doing just that. He had had a bad experience of humans since he had been uprooted from the only home he had ever known; it made good cat-sense that he should be extremely cautious about ever trusting a human again. He had established the fact that the human associated with the regularly supplied food did him no harm, but obviously to enter the house except for food was a risk; he could be trapped again, pushed into a basket, seized by strange hands, shut up. He had to be sure that he could come and go freely in this house. It made sense.

The weather became very cold. The lily pond froze, harder and harder. I would go out each morning and break the ice, for the benefit of the fish, but after a few days the ice became too thick to break, and I was melting the ice on the bird bath twice a day. On February 14 I went out as usual in the morning with a kettle of hot water for dealing with the bird bath, and with a bowl of bread for the birds. I had taken only a few steps across the loggia when the honey-coloured cat came round the house. He stopped and looked up at me. Now it was he who beseeched.

'Wow!' he said. 'I'm hungry, and I'm cold.'

I put down the kettle and the bowl of bread and knelt down beside him and stroked his head.

Sammy, the little feller, common or garden, *gamin* . . .

Before Sammy there was Lucy, the devil-cat, beautiful and indifferent

On hot days Sammy 'lies up' in the garden, like the tiger in the jungle

'Come *in*,' I said.

He pushed his head against my hand.

'You're my Valentine,' I said.

He tried to get into my lap as I knelt there; I picked him up and carried him into the house. He purred and purred. I carried him upstairs to the study and put him down on the divan and stroked him – and he hissed and dabbed out at me, his claws out. Then pushed his head against me and went on purring. He was the cat who had come in from the cold; but he was also, it seemed, a mixed-up kid. The end was not yet. Not by a long chalk.

Chapter Four

THAT St Valentine's Day we began a new chapter, Sammy and I. The first had been difficult; the second was not less so. He was in the house now; domesticated, occupying chairs, stretching out in front of the fire; this house was his home now, no longer to be sniffed as strange and suspicious, no longer to be yelled at as a trap, and escaped from, but accepted – his place. But in this place humans had to be kept in their place, and to this self-protective end they had still to be hissed at, clawed, and dabbed at. Because he had taken up residence with humans it was not to be assumed that he was subordinate to them; he most definitely was not. There was, in fact, only this human, and Tim and sometimes other friends at week-ends. They were all charmed by the handsome cat, but they were all warned not to touch him. He would get into their laps, and instinctively they would caress him – and get bitten for their pains.

'He's maladjusted,' I would explain, apologetically, going off for the antiseptic ointment for their wounds.

My daughter, who had been opposed to my having him, for purely practical considerations, would inquire, sardonically, 'How's the cat? Has he bitten anyone lately?'

My little granddaughter, Catherine, who had loved him from the word go and who had disregarded my warnings not to stroke him, wept when he scratched her – not from pain but from grief.

During the first week of his residence I would walk all round the furniture to avoid coming within reach of the paw he would reach out to take a swipe at my ankles as I passed. We had great tussles over the swing chair at my typing desk. He fancied it and would squeeze in behind me when I occupied it, trying to oust me, and hissing when I in turn tried to oust him, and clawing at me when, finally, exasperated, I would forcibly eject him. Occasionally I would relinquish it to him, take an ordinary chair, turn the typewriter round, and sit at the end of the desk instead of facing it. But it was inconvenient to me not to be able to swing round to the telephone, the encyclopaedia, and the various things I needed on the telephone table, and eventually I would pick him up and dump him somewhere else, regardless of the hissing and scratching. At the end of a week my hands were covered with scratches and bites. At the end of the second week I began to feel I had had enough. To the vet who had had him, and who knew of the five weeks of watching and waiting for him to come and 'live in', and who had inquired how I was getting on with the Ilford tiger, as he called him, I replied that I despaired of ever rehabilitating this cat; that I felt he had been too deeply disturbed by his upheaval ever to become again the domesticated animal he once was when he lived in Ilford and bore good-naturedly with the attentions of three children at once. I began to feel, I said, that I couldn't cope; that I would be driven to having him put down . . . I resorted to that euphemism unable to bring myself to say have him destroyed, killed – which was too monstrous a crime to state explicitly. And yet . . .

The vet, however, had no such scruples. (He was a dog man, himself.) When there were so many charming creatures available as pets, he urged, why should I saddle myself for ten years or more with this hissing, clawing, biting little savage?

He missed the point, of course; I had never wanted a 'pet'; I have this thing about cats; this *empathy* with the creatures; and this was a cat that had wanted a home, and who had got into my lap that fatal day at lunch in the Ilford house and pushed his little wet nose against my hands and said so plainly, '*You* take me! Let me come and live with *you*!' I hadn't wanted another cat, but when you have this 'thing', what can you do when a cat comes wrapping its beauty, its *catness*, round your heart and mind? What can you *do*?

The vet, being a dog man, couldn't understand what it is cats do to the cat people, but his well-meant but uncomprehending counsel shocked me out of the defeatism into which I was falling. Shocked me, too, into being shocked at myself.

I had telephoned Tim.

'I can't cope with this cat,' I had declared. 'Tonight when I tried to get him out of my chair he jumped on to my back. I'm scared of him! I'll have to give him to the vet.'

'Oh no!' He was horrified. 'That would be terrible!'

'*You* haven't got to live with him,' I said bitterly.

He pleaded, 'I'm sure it's only a matter of time. He has to readjust. You were so patient all those weeks. He's not a vicious cat. You said yourself how good he was with the children. He's had a bad experience. He has to learn to trust people again.'

He was right, of course. I knew in my heart he was right. But patience is not inexhaustible. Mine, anyhow. And he was making it hard for me, that little tiger-cat – who seemed, then, so much more tiger than cat. Than domestic cat, that is.

I don't know, really, when this phase ended. But there came a point at which I could pass him without him dabbing out at my ankles, and then a point at which it was safe to stroke him, and he hissed less often, and then in time not at all – or almost not at all; to this day he will sometimes hiss if annoyed, such as when someone in whose lap he has been sitting decides to get up, or he is removed from a seat requisitioned by a human. But it was four years before anyone dared to rub his lovely belly when he rolled over to expose it, legs in air. Now it is even safe to let him back-pedal with his hind-legs on to your hands and take your hand in his mouth, for though his teeth fasten on he never drives them in. His play is rough, and it doesn't do to keep on with it too long, for he becomes over-excited and his claws come out; it is a case of so far and no farther – beyond that point he suddenly goes wild.

But four years ago no liberties at all were possible, and no play except with a rolled up newspaper, which he would claw savagely.

In those days even Tim, his staunch defender, said once, dabbing the blood from his hand, 'He's not a proper cat! He's something escaped from a zoo!'

But he's a proper cat, all right, and, as it was to turn out, much more properly a cat than I'd bargained for.

Chapter Five

ALTHOUGH I did know the zoological fact of life that the whole cat tribe is nocturnal I was all the same startled when Sammy's former owner told me that he slept out at nights.

'In this bitter weather?' I said.

'The children have made him a little house,' she explained.

I was startled because for sixteen years I had conscientiously kept Lucy in at nights, often going to some trouble to get her in, telling myself that the Great Cat is wild and the domestic cat many degrees removed from that state. When I knew for certain that I was going to have this male cat it pleased me to think that now he would never sleep out again; there would be the warm kitchen in winter and anywhere he chose to roost in the summer. But, conditioned from kittenhood to being a wanderer in the night, Sammy had quite other ideas; he had no intention of changing his nocturnal habits because he had been forced to change habitat. Although he came in that St Valentine's Day, and spent the entire day in the house, towards evening he sat up and gave himself an extensive wash-and-brush-up; then he rolled around a little, inviting admiration, and after a little play, with a few appropriate remarks from me · 'He is a *most* beautiful pussy-*cat*!' – he got up and went to the door. We went downstairs together; the door into the dining-room being open he marched in and crossed the room to the loggia door and waited for me to open it. I let him out, then went back into the kitchen for his supper; when I returned with the tray he was sitting on the mat outside the door, alert, watching, listening. I put the tray down against the wall of the house, folded some blankets into an old armchair, watched for a moment that he settled to his food, then went in, closing the door behind me. When I went down in the morning at half-past eight he was in the armchair; he got up, stretched, and came into the house for breakfast and spent the day indoors, with me in the study, and in the evening repeated the washing and rolling ritual; the routine was established.

Several times on very bad wet nights I have opened the loggia door to check that he's safely there in the dry, and inquire whether he'd like to come in. Only once has he been there, and I have worried, picturing him crouching in inadequate shelter somewhere, but in the morning he has been there – and dry. Where he gets to I will never know. The only occasion he was there was a night when the snow was blowing in all directions and sweeping into the loggia; he was glad, then, to come in and spend the rest of the night in the house.

There have been a few nights of wind and rain when he has evinced no desire to go out and has taken his supper with me in the study, and remained there at midnight when I have gone to bed. On other equally bad nights, when I have encouraged him to stay in, he has resisted the idea and demanded to be let out. Often on cold winter nights going out for coal for the kitchen boiler I have found him on the doorstep of the back door; he has come in, then, reluctantly, when coaxed, but has never settled, making it plain that to stay in of his own accord is one thing, but to be enticed in, when he was all right where he was on the cold doorstep, quite another.

I imposed my will on Lucy; now I know better; I accept that a cat knows its own business best, and Sammy does as he pleases.

The 'cat books' dealing with the care and management of cats, urge the importance of 'keeping your cat in at night', lest it be stolen, run over, or suffer from the damp and cold of the night air – overlooking the fact of the cat's higher blood temperature and its specially grown winter coat. As to being stolen or run over, that is a hazard of town and city life, and not confined to night time. Cats do get stolen in some areas, and in any area, if they venture into the streets, they are liable to be run over. Fortunately, cats with their nine lives have a remarkable capacity for survival. Lucy seldom left her own private jungle; when she did it was only for another garden; Sammy, being male, is more adventurous, and I returned from posting my letters one evening to see him marching off up the road. A few houses along he jumped the gate into the front garden. Alarmed, I went in after him and carried him home – and as soon as I set him down in the house he made for an open window and went off out again. I followed him and he went round the house, down the tradesmen's entrance at the side, under the gate, and out again on to the pavement. I went out to the road and watched him once again jump the gate into the front garden of the house a few doors along. What he wanted there I have no idea, and it was not my business. He came back later for a meal, then went out again. He was in his chair on the loggia in the morning. In time he developed the habit of coming round to the side door of the house and jumping on to the coal bin outside the kitchen window; sometimes he sits there for hours – it is a good look-out post the length of the tradesmen's entrance; sometimes he goes there at midnight and waits for me to come into the kitchen, which I do, around that time, when I have finished my night's work (I am myself as nocturnal as a cat), to put on a kettle for a hot water bottle, or get myself a glass of milk; when he is waiting for me, and not merely sitting there sniffing the night and guarding his territory, he comes close to the window, and when I lift the corner of the curtain presses his face against the pane. It is my cue then to let him in for a late-night snack, which, unless he has had an exceptionally large supper – such as six ounces of raw minced beef – I invariably do, giving it to him on the loggia, to which, when I pick up the tray, he invariably leads me. On these occasions he is not much inclined for breakfast next day and sometimes doesn't bother to get up when I open the door. Most mornings, after he has break-fasted in the kitchen, he comes up to my bedroom, to which I have taken my breakfast tray, *The Times*, and the morning's mail. He then jumps up on to the bed and, purring loudly, treads with his front paws on the arm of the old hairy dressing-gown I put on specially to oblige him. No one seems to know what this treading – which some people call 'making pastry' – signifies. Lucy would do it on any woollen garment when she was in the mood; Sammy will only do it on this dressing-gown so long as I am wearing it; if I merely leave it on the bed for him he is not interested. There is a theory that this treading is some kind of hangover from kittenhood and the kneading of the mother's flanks to encourage the flow of milk, but this seems to me far-fetched. Whatever it may signify, however, it is obviously pleasurable, always accompanied by loud purring.

Though purring, according to Dr Méry, is not necessarily

a sign of pleasure, but a purely physical reflex. We know very little about it, he says, and he has known cats purr on the operating table, which, as he says, can hardly be a manifestation of pleasure. Until I read this in Dr Méry's book it puzzled me that Sammy purred when he was miserably ill, in circumstances I will describe later. He had absolutely no reason to purr as an expression of well-being, but purr he did, very loudly, and the vet told him, 'you're making too much noise,' by which he meant that his condition was abnormal. Dr Méry, strangely, says nothing about 'treading' in his discussion of behaviour.

Sammy moved in, then, in his own time, and on his own conditions. He established his routine, and it suits me well enough. He goes out just at the time I am ready to settle down for my night's work; Sir Walter Scott, apparently, liked his cat on his writing desk; apart from the fact that my typing desk is far too small to accommodate the type-writer, my papers, and the cat, I anyhow prefer to be alone when working, even to the exclusion of so silent and unobtrusive a creature as a cat. The routine is fine, but every now and then it is broken by bouts of absenteeism, lasting from forty-eight hours to five days and nights. The last one lasted eight days, but that was no mere absenteeism but a disaster with an incredible dénouement.

The spells of absenteeism occur in what I have called the 'cat months' of March and November, that is to say at the onset of spring and the onset of winter. That there should be restlessness at the time of the spring equinox is under-standable; much less readily understandable is a similar restlessness with the onset of the cold weather. Dr Méry writes about the cat's love of warmth, but says nothing about the effect on its behaviour under the seasonal impact of cold. Lucy first came into season in mid-winter, and set out across a snowy landscape in search of *l'amour*, leaving the safety of this garden for the first time, but relentlessly driven. 'Restless as a tomcat in March,' they say, but it seems that something also happens in November, with the first sting of frost on the air. All through the summer there will have been no cats around, nor in the mellow days of September and October, then suddenly it's winter and there are cats again – thickly clad and handsome in their winter coats, invading territory, prowling, seeking, and there are scuffles and caterwaulings in the night. I cite no authority for this; I write of what I have observed.

But why this cat, a eunuch, should be seized with restlessness in early spring, and with the onset of winter, I found extremely puzzling. To friends who were similarly puzzled I would say, helplessly, that there must be some deep ineradicable impulse that neutering didn't dispose of. One or two of the more ribald of them observed pointedly that you'd never know he was neutered, for he seemed to be remarkably well-equipped . . .

Well, yes, to be sure, but 'They don't castrate a three-year-old cat to neuter it,' I would say, knowledgeably. 'There's something else they do . . . '

I could only assume it was so. He had been at the vet's best part of a week, and on the telephone they'd said, 'He's had his operation.'

Which was precisely what made his periodic bouts of absenteeism so puzzling. Then the longest bout of all, and two astonishing discoveries.

Chapter Six

INVARIABLY when he has 'gone missing' for several days and nights Sammy returns a wounded warrior, with scratches about his head and ears, as likely as not a wounded forepaw, and once an obviously bitten hindleg. He will come limping in, but not complaining of anything except hunger. Once he limped in and quite angrily demanded food, positively shouting at me to produce it, and quickly. Like a terrible American child I once saw and heard on a ship who, when asked by his mother what he would like for breakfast, declared loudly, 'I wanna steak! An' I wan' it quick!'

During Sammy's protracted absence I had longed for the sight of his golden body coming round the door of my study, which I had all the time left open for him; now that he was back and shouting at me all that was forgotten and I felt annoyed; resentful.

'All *right*!' I said. 'It's not *my* fault if you go off for days on end, is it? And look at the state you're in – all scratches, and dot-and-carry! Where have you *been* all this time?'

Just like an overwrought, scolding mother, whose relief at Junior's safe return gets swamped by irritation at his impenitence over all the worry he has caused her. If only he would say he was sorry, say where he had been, ask forgiveness. But Sammy was not sorry; he was only hungry – and tired, and battered. As to where he had been I could not even guess. I quite literally hadn't a clue.

Always on such occasions when he has groomed himself, after eating, he settles in one of his 'places' and sleeps and sleeps, curled up tight, head to tail. His places in the study are at the end of the divan – always the same end, even the same spot – under my desk, on a chair beside the desk, in my swing chair if he can nab it – but when he returns from his wanderings he is not disposed to contest the rights to this chair if it's occupied and any of his accepted places will do. The important thing, once hunger has been taken care of, is sleep.

The amount of sleep cats go in for is prodigious. Sometimes it seems as though they sleep most of their lives away. Very often when I have had occasion to be absent from home for a long day, as much as twelve hours, I have left Sammy asleep on my bed only to find him still there when I got back in the evening; usually he comes downstairs at the sound of the front door opening, wreathes himself around my legs, purring loudly, but when a few kind words have been exchanged leads me to the kitchen door, sometimes standing up on his hindlegs and reaching up to the handle in his eagerness for the door to open. As soon as we are in the kitchen he leads the way to the larder. Hoping for his company, since I have been out all day, I have put his food and milk on a tray and set off out of the kitchen and up the stairs to my study, thinking he might take his supper there and stay around for a while, but he always stops at the foot of the stairs, and when I turn and invite him to come up he says No, quite firmly.

'No,' he says. 'You're late back and I'm already overdue out there in the night!'

I go back down the stairs and meekly set the tray down in the kitchen, and when he has eaten he has his usual wash-

and-brush-up and stalks off out. It is my experience that cats like company but that they like it on their own terms, and the night is for wandering in, not to waste sitting around with humans. There are, I suppose, cats that docilely stay in all night and every night, but the Proper Cat goes out, as designed by Nature, just as the tiger, who has slept all day, stirs in the jungle at sundown, sits up and licks himself, and sets out on his beat, patrolling his territory, hunting, seeking.

Even after she was spayed Lucy went out at night; most nights around midnight I would get her in by calling to her; most nights, but not always. She was no longer a Proper Cat, but still *cat* enough to love the night. Sammy has had the freedom of the night from early cathood. In the mornings when he comes in his eyes are still dark with night, the pupils round and black; as the day wears on they stop down like the lens of a camera, to mere slits, and the lines of Yeats's lovely cat poem come to mind:

> '*Minnaloushe creeps through the grass,*
> *Alone, important and wise,*
> *And lifts to the changing moon*
> *His changing eyes.*'

Sometimes after he has gone out at night I am disturbed in my work by the most hideous sounds from the garden; the terrible, blood-curdling sounds of cats at war with each other. I have rushed down and out and there has been Sammy confronting another cat, his hackles up, and dreadful strangulated sounds coming from his throat, and the other cat hypnotized. I have never read anything about this horrible thing male cats do to each other, but have many times witnessed it. Perhaps hypnotize is not the right word;

46

perhaps paralyze is the better word, for what happens is that one cat stands, swishing its tail, uttering these horrible strangulated sounds, and the other cat crouches transfixed. The sight has always filled me with a peculiar kind of horror – and a kind of blind anger; I have flapped and shooed, and this breaks the evil spell and the immobilized cat is suddenly released and rushes off, pursued, savagely, by the other cat; there ensues a fierce scuffle, with hissing and spitting and yells – from which the aggressor cat emerges in a minute or two with great dignity and something very like smugness – an air of '*That*'ll larn him!'

After these affrays Sammy will consent to come in for a while, but never for long; he still has business in the night, to do with patrolling and defending territory.

Sometimes territory has to be defended in broad daylight. I was sitting on a garden seat with Sammy one warm sunny afternoon, Sammy luxuriously on a cushion – we had been having after lunch coffee together, the coffee for me, the cream for him – when suddenly he sat up, alert, intent, gazing up the narrow path between the rhododendrons, a few yards from the lily pond by which we sat. Nothing alien was in sight, and I could hear nothing except a light twitter of birds – and Sammy is totally uninterested in birds – and then through the sunlight and shadows emerged a young Siamese cat, small, delicately coloured, exquisitely graceful; it halted at the end of the path, above some steps and looked across at us a few yards away. Sammy stared incredulously; I had the feeling he had never seen that kind of cat before. He stared and the young Siamese stared, as though surprised to come upon a human being and a cat at the end of his walk; there was that moment of mutual astonishment, and then Sammy leapt from the seat and flew across the grass beside the pond, up the two steps at the far side, across a paved path, and up two more steps to the path between the rhododendrons – along which the Siamese was fleeing at the same arrow-from-a-bow speed. The Siamese made it to the compost-heap corner beyond the rhododendrons, jumped a high fence and escaped, Sammy not being interested to pursue beyond his own territory. Having seen the intruder off the premises he rejoined me on the seat beside the lily pond, but he did not relax; until that astonishing apparition he had been dozing in the warm sunshine; now he was wide awake, alert, watching.

That poor young Siamese, how was he to know there was, in Carl Van Vechten's words, 'a tiger in the house'?*

The analogy of the tiger was strongly with me that day, for in the morning Sammy had marched into the house with a baby squirrel in his mouth. My first horrified impulse was to get it away from him, just as I had often taken away from Lucy the birds she was always catching in her youth. I tried to make Sammy drop the squirrel, but he refused, and I failed to open his mouth; then I saw that the squirrel was dead. In irrational anger I then picked the little tiger up and flung him out into the yard with his kill still in his mouth. He crouched for a moment, his ears back, his tail swishing, angrily, then, finding that I did not come after him relaxed, dropped the squirrel, and for a few minutes played with it, tossing it up into the air, whirling round after it as only the day before I had watched him crazily spinning round after his own tail, with a great show of anger when, after pouncing on it, he straightened himself only to turn his head to see the damn thing still waving

* *The Tiger in the House*, 1936, New York.

48

Frisky and Lucy; at first he was nervous of approaching her

Lucy; from the low roof she would go up over a steep tiled gable

Frisky . . . from half-way up a cherry tree would scour the landscape hopefully

Sammy . . . is beautiful, not in the elegant Siamese fashion, but *wildly* . . .

at his rear – when the performance would start all over again.

The play with the dead squirrel went on for a few minutes, then he tore into its belly with his sharp little fangs and got down to eating it. I had a momentary revulsion and thought I must take it away from him, then overcame that with the reflection that after all I occasionally gave him raw meat, and the only difference was that this was meat he had killed for himself, as designed by Nature, and a good deal fresher than anything I got him from the butcher's. It was, after all, his 'kill', and he was entitled to the enjoyment of it. I watched him for a few minutes, devouring the innards, then went indoors and left him to it and set about preparing my own lunch – which that day was vegetarian, in contrast to the carnivorous feast outside. I reflected, poaching my eggs, that human beings were, after all, not intended by Nature to be carnivorous, having neither the right teeth nor intestines for it.

When I looked again Sammy had finished with the squirrel and was sitting up washing himself; there was still some blood on his face. He stopped washing and watched when I scooped up the remains of the squirrel – mostly bloody fur – rolling it all up into newspaper. I did not examine the mess closely, but the head seemed to be missing. When I had cleaned up the spot he got up and examined it, sniffing, then finding nothing there resumed his washing.

I carried the remains up to the bonfire heap; by the time the cremation was under way Sammy was sleeping it all off on the seat beside the lily pond.

This incident raises the whole question of the proper food for cats, and that considerable authority, Brian Vesey-

FitzGerald, declares emphatically,* 'The most important food for a cat is raw meat.' He points out that it is the animal's natural food, and says that 'ideally a cat should have some raw lean meat, preferably beef or horse, every day.' He recommends giving a cat hunks of rabbit, fur and all – adding that most people think this 'crude and shocking', but that the cat does not. All except the most pampered of cats knows, as he says, what to do with a hunk of rabbit in its natural state – cats after all hunt and kill wild rabbits when they get the chance, and eat their kill. Cats also know what to do with chicken heads, and though 'boudoir' cats which have led very sheltered lives are, he says, 'sometimes a little surprised by their first chicken head . . . even the most pampered pet puss tumbles to the idea pretty quickly. Worldly cats think chicken heads heaven.'

A cat eats its kill bones and all; it is cooked bones which are dangerous, because they splinter. Vesey-FitzGerald, however, believes that fish should be cooked for a cat, and the bones carefully removed. My experience, however, is that cats like raw fish very much, and during Lucy's serious illness, when she had the septic uterus, following the birth of the monster kitten, and was like to die and had not eaten for days, it was an offering of raw fish which started her eating again and on the road to recovery. Sammy likes a lightly boiled egg; some cats like raw eggs, which are probably even better for them. Cats are not difficult to feed; like humans they like some things better than others. Sammy is crazy about fish and chicken and is an infernal nuisance when I am cooking either – in fact, if he meets me with my shopping bag when I have brought either home he begins pestering before I have even unpacked. That he

* In *The Domestic Cat*, 1969.

may have had a whole tin of pet food for breakfast makes no difference – he had consumed a whole tin of one of the best of the pet foods for breakfast the day he had the young squirrel for lunch. Vesey-FitzGerald is not opposed to pet foods; he keeps a stock of them himself, and acknowledges that a cat fed entirely on tinned foods can be 'just as healthy, just as physically fit, as the cat living on more natural foods', but he points out that it is not that the best of the tinned foods are wholesome and nourishing and beneficial to the cat that has led to their enormous success, but that they are convenient for humans – 'It is so much easier, and so much quicker, and so much cleaner, to open a tin than it is to chop up a rabbit or steam and bone fish,' and 'marvellous to be able to save time and trouble with a clear conscience; to know that your cat does not suffer because you have clean hands.' Whether such very clean hands are good in this context is a matter for the individual, and Vesey-FitzGerald is well aware that 'for many people the tin-opener is the only answer'.

I find myself with no very strong views on the subject. It is obviously better for both animals and humans to eat as far as possible as Nature intended, but if we can remain healthy by eating what we like rather than what is naturally good for us there seems to me no reason for making a fetish of 'health foods'. Because, for example, raw vegetables – grated carrot, chopped cabbage – are dietetically better than cooked vegetables seems to me no reason why one should not also enjoy cabbage or carrots cooked, deliciously, in butter; they will have lost some of their goodness by being cooked, but not all.

The same principle, I think applies to the feeding of domestic animals. More often than not it is convenient to open a tin, but it is good occasionally to allow the animal its natural food. For the first three years of his life, before he moved in with me, Sammy was fed on tinned pet food, and one of the less good ones at that, and he grew to be a fine handsome cat. With me he learned that there were better things, and now the pet food on which he was brought up is the one he likes least; he will eat it, but he never demands the second helping that finishes the tin, and if the second half is kept till next day is inclined to sniff at it and reject it – 'Oh, *that*! It wasn't even all that good when first opened!' He will take it *faute de mieux*. I give it to him when he has eaten specially well the day before, such as when I cook a chicken, or go to the fish shop and in addition to what I buy for myself bring back half a pound of coley for him – six ounces of which he will eat in one go. He will then have the rest for breakfast, but for supper that day – if he wants any – there is only the inferior brand of pet food; but sometimes he is content with a little milk, and there he breaks the natural law by much preferring evaporated tinned milk to fresh milk – as many cats seem to.

But a cat does not break a natural law, but, on the contrary, confirms one, when it drinks from a murky pond whilst refusing the 'pure' piped water put down for it. I have never had a cat that would drink water other than from the garden pond – and have never lost a goldfish to a cat. Cats are reputed to fish, but I have never met one that did.

Chapter Seven

A T first Sammy's bouts of absenteeism worried me; I would have fantasies of him lying injured somewhere, unable to drag himself back home; or locked in someone's garage and the owners gone on holiday; I never thought of him being lost, because cats don't get lost, being possessed of that astonishing sixth sense which those who have done research on it call 'psi-trailing', though for Dr Méry the sixth sense is the cat's 'second sight', or extra-sensory perception. I cannot find, myself, that E.S.P. in the cat is really scientifically documented, but the contention that cats find their way back home over huge distances does appear to be supported by abundant evidence. Examples of such cases are constantly reported in the British press, and Dr Méry cites some verifiable French examples, and says that 'some stupefying cases have been studied by serious American researchers', and gives particulars of experiments carried out in America, and also in Germany, which are truly astonishing. Brian Vesey-FitzGerald, in *The Domestic Cat*, says that he has a 'long list, going back almost forty years, of fully authenticated instances of cats finding their way home over long distances and across unknown country'. He gives a number of remarkable instances, and says that he has many other records of a similar nature, not only from Britain but from the United States and all over Europe. He calls it the homing instinct, and says that when a cat which has been happily settled in a new home for a year or more suddenly sets off for its old home clearly memory operates, and that there can be no doubt that some cats have very long memories indeed.

Yet when Sammy has gone off I have never really believed he has decided to return to his old home; I always thought that because he had stayed for a week with a vet before being finally brought to me he would have become confused as to sense of direction . . . I had not then read either Dr Méry or Vesey-FitzGerald on the subject; if I had I should have been a great deal more worried than I was.

The absences became progressively longer, as though he were each time exploring further afield – thirty-six hours, forty-eight hours, seventy-two hours; then a five-day absence, during which I became really worried. When he returned after that I thought I would never again worry about him, as I knew now, I told myself, that he would always come back. So that the next time when he had been gone five days I was sure he would return that night; when he didn't I felt uneasy.

I had been away for a week, and when I got back in the late afternoon he was not there, and the food left down for him by the person who had been living in the house in my absence was not touched. When he had not returned by midnight I left the door open for him on to the loggia when I went to bed. But in the morning he was still not there, and he was not there for day after day, and after the fifth day, on which I had counted on his return, I began to be worried. It was late May, not the 'cat time' of the year, and this added to my anxiety. Tim was convinced that Sammy had left home from lack of company; cats like company, he insisted, and I had left Sammy with someone who not only did not much care for cats but who was out all day and every day, leaving here early in the morning and not returning until late at night, and once – perhaps more than once – not returning overnight at all. I refused to believe he would leave a place where there was always food, whether I was there or not, and where he had by then lived for over three years. By the sixth day I was really depressed, convinced that he had been stolen, or picked up poison, or, as various people suggested, 'got shut in somewhere'. Mournfully when I telephoned Tim I told him, 'We shall never see that little Pushy-cat again!' We had nicknamed him Pushy-cat because of his habit of pushing his head against one's face when picked up. Tim invariably addressed him as Pushkin, and if he can be said to answer to any name it is that. Night and day I left the door open for him. By the seventh day I was wondering, morosely, how long I would go on doing so, in the forlorn hope of his return. I wrote in my journal that I was 'now quite sure the little feller will come no more'. I felt miserable. I hadn't felt so miserable since Lucy died. Depressed, I felt, and low; rockbottom low.

The eighth day was Sunday, and Tim was here; before another friend arrived a few hours later he was determined to search a new housing estate near here in search of Sammy. He could so easily have gone there, he said, cutting across the tennis court beyond this garden he could reach it without ever touching a road, and for all we knew that was his regularly nightly beat. I couldn't see why he should be more likely to go there than anywhere else; the fact was we had no idea where he had gone – where he ever went. But a search has to start somewhere, and there was, really, nowhere else to search, every corner of the garden having been combed.

Tim went off and was away for an hour or more. When he got back he was low; rockbottom low. He had inquired of children playing in the road, but none had seen a big ginger cat; one child had told him, offhandedly, that there were no cats around there; everyone had dogs. He had inquired of men washing their cars and mowing their lawns; he had talked with a gardener, who had been sympathetic and to whom he had given my name and address, and who had promised to let me know if he found out anything in the gardens in which he worked in the district. Only this gardener had been at all interested or sympathetic; no one else had cared; it was a dog district . . .

He had peered into gardens and garages, and he had called as he peered.

'People must have thought I was mad, peering in everywhere, and calling. The gardener young man asked me his name, and I said it was Sammy, but I told him he was usually just called Pussy-cat. He was a nice, friendly young man. He had a cat himself, he said. He liked cats. Nobody else over there seemed to!'

'Well,' I said, firmly, 'Sammy-cat isn't there. Let me get you a gin-and-tonic. It'll do you good.'

I went out and got the drink and came back and set it in front of him.

He regarded it without interest.

'He was such a nice little feller,' he lamented.

'Oh, for God's sake!' I said.

Irritably, impatiently, I said it, being so damn miserable myself. I poured myself a drink, twice the size of his.

When the other friend came, in the afternoon, he inquired, 'Has the cat come back?'

'No,' I said, and added, resolutely, 'He's not likely to come back now. He's gone for good this time.'

'You never know,' the friend suggested, helpfully. 'I had a friend whose cat went away for three weeks and then came back.'

'A neutered cat?'

'Well, no. I suppose that does make a difference . . . '

'All the difference in the world,' I assured him. 'This cat had no reason to go away.'

'He's been away before – I think you said?'

'Never for as long as this.'

'He's dead,' Tim insisted. 'If he was alive he'd have come back by now.'

Because I thought he was right and I couldn't bear it I said harshly, 'We don't know. We'll never know. All we know is that he's gone. Let's talk about something else . . . '

We talked of other things. We had tea, we had drinks, we had supper; it was a pleasant enough evening, three old friends together. The guests left at about ten, and I washed up and came upstairs to the study and sat down at the typewriter, too tired for work, but there are always letters awaiting answering in the wire basket. They come in every day, regular as the tides. But I couldn't concentrate and switched on the radio. A literary gentleman was talking about his tastes in prose and poetry, with the greatest pleasure, don't you know, but his tastes were not my tastes, and with the greatest pleasure I switched off and went back to the typewriter. I typed the date and Dear So-and-So. Then paused; this was going to be one of those difficult letters; how to tell a man politely not only that you profoundly disagree with him but think he's talking non-sense . . .

I frowned at the paper in the machine, then looked up – and there in front of the bookshelves by the door stood the little feller – or his ghost, a gaunt, thin honey-coloured cat with sunken flanks and his backbone a ridge. We looked at each other.

'Wow,' he said. 'I'm back,' then began to cough.

I got up and went over to him and picked him up, a little bag of bones. He purred and coughed and purred, and coughed and coughed.

I carried him downstairs to the kitchen and opened a tin for him and warmed some milk, put both on his tray and set it down in front of him on the floor. He took a mouthful of the food and immediately brought it up, and coughed and coughed.

I picked him up again and brought him up here and he lay on the floor coughing and writhing. It seemed to me he was going to die unless something could be done for him. It was past eleven, but I rang the vet; I didn't expect him to be there at that time of night, and he wasn't, but one of the veterinary nurses answered and I described the cat's condition to her. She said to give him some glucose – as though everyone just naturally had glucose in the house – and when I said I hadn't any said to boil some water and stir some white of egg into it and try him with that, and let them know how he was in the morning. I did as she said but he wouldn't touch it. I put him on the chair beside my desk and he settled down on the cushion and after a little while stopped coughing and folded himself up and went to sleep.

I rang Tim and told him that Sammy was back, but that

he was in very bad shape – a ghost cat, I said, unable to keep food down and continuously coughing.

Tim suggested that perhaps he was exhausted and would be all right when he had rested; he had perhaps travelled a long way in a starved condition. We discussed trying to find another vet who might come at that late hour, but decided against it. I should leave some milk down for him when I went to bed and see how he was in the morning.

I went to bed reflecting that if he died in the night he would anyhow die at home, and it was an end of the anxiety of wondering and wondering where he was. It had been a very nervously exhausting week. But he was back, the little feller, and that was everything. If he was still alive in the morning it would only be a matter of getting a vet to give him something for his cough and then building him up again, I thought.

But in that I was wrong.

Chapter Eight

I was half afraid to go into the study in the morning; if that emaciated, honey-coloured little body should be stretched out dead . . .

But he was on the chair where I had left him, still curled up, head to tail. When I went over to him he sat up; I knelt down beside him and we rubbed heads together; he purred loudly – unnaturally loudly. I went away and got him some food; he jumped down from the chair and took a mouthful – and it came straight back. I tried to coax him with some milk, but he wouldn't have it. I made tea and toast for myself and took it up to my room, and as was his wont he joined me there, folding himself up close to me and resting a paw on the back of my hand, and always that unnaturally loud purring.

When I was bathed and dressed I walked up the road to the shops and at the chemist's bought him some chicken essence, which from my experience with Lucy I knew a sick cat will take when it will take nothing else. He was still on my bed when I got back and I ladled a spoonful of the delicious jelly on to a saucer and offered it to him; he sniffed it, and to my surprise and disappointment refused it. A cat that will refuse chicken essence is a very sick cat indeed. There was obviously nothing for it but to telephone the vet. Then suddenly I remembered that although I did not know his name there was a vet who lived just up the road from me. I knew this because some months ago I had found a little Scottie wandering about in my garden, and though he was a very friendly little dog he was also not very bright, for when I showed him the front gate he showed no inclination to go through it. I then looked at his collar and found inscribed thereon a telephone number. Sammy meanwhile had come down the front path and was extremely indignant at finding a *dog*, of all outrages, on his territory; his ears went back, his hackles went up, and he hissed and spat with the utmost vehemence. I know better than to touch a cat with its hackles up so I enticed the Scottie into the outside W.C. and shut him in, then went back into the house to telephone.

I said to the voice that answered, 'I have your Scottie here. Will you come and get him? I have no car.'

The voice said, unhelpfully, 'This is the surgery.'

I said, 'I am ringing—' and repeated the number.

'That's right,' the voice said, 'but there's no one here. Mr' – I could not make out the name – 'has gone home.'

'If you'll give me the number I'll ring there.'

The voice gave me a number.

I exclaimed, 'That's a Wimbledon number. I am speaking from Wimbledon. What is the address?'

The voice gave me a number in my own road.

'How very odd,' I said, 'I live in that road!'

I rang the number to make sure there was someone at home.

A female voice replied, repeating the number.

'I live across the road from you,' I said, 'and I have your Scottie.'

'We wondered where he had got to,' the voice said.

Slightly nettled I said, 'Would you like to come and get him?'

'I'm baby-sitting,' the voice said. 'They're both out.'

'I'll come over,' I said.

I tied a string to the Scottie's tartan collar and led him down the tradesmen's entrance and up the road. The baby-sitter waited at the gate – young, unremarkable. She bent down and patted her knees, encouragingly, when she sighted us, and the Scottie responded by wagging his tail and quickening his pace.

She said again, as I handed over, 'We wondered where he'd got to.'

'He hadn't got far,' I said, feeling vaguely irritated, and then, a little sharply, no thanks being forthcoming, 'Whose house is this?'

'The vet's,' she said, as though there was only one in the district.

When Sammy refused the chicken essence I remembered the tiresome little incident and decided to go across the road to the vet whose dog I had returned but whose name I did not know, and whose surgery number I no longer had.

The door was opened by an attractive young woman. I explained that I lived down the road and had a very sick cat. She said, friendlily, that her husband was at the surgery but would be back at lunch time and she would tell him.

He came in the early afternoon; he was young, Scottish, and pleasant, a newcomer to the district. Sammy did not bat a whisker when the young man pushed a thermometer up his rectum, applied a stethoscope to his chest, gave him an antibiotic injection. He had pneumonia, he said. He would come again tomorrow.

I said, mournfully, seeing him off. 'Such a little bag of bones he is now! He used to be such a fine handsome cat—'

'He will be again,' he said.

'What shall I feed him?' I asked.

'Anything he will take.'

'Nothing stays down.'

'Try him with a lightly boiled egg.'

Sammy had a big sleep after the injection. When he awakened from it I gave him the egg, very wet, and it stayed down. Later I gave him some of the chicken essence and it too stayed down. But he still coughed. I wanted to keep him in that night, but towards evening he became restless; it was his going-out time, and the night called – not only with the cry of the owls but with those minute sounds that only the nocturnal animal hears. I shut him in the dining-room with the door open to the loggia and the grill-gates closed across it – he goes easily through this grill. I thought he might spend the night in a chair in there, content with just looking out into the night through the grill gates, but when I went in at midnight he was not there. He had gone out through the grill into the darkness, a wanderer in the night even with pneumonia . . .

What would he find to do out there, for God's sake, I asked myself. Hadn't he had enough of wandering? Well, evidently not. A cat is a cat is a cat. It was a fine June night, warm. He had spent last night in the house, but now with an antibiotic injection in his veins, and a little food in his belly, he could face the night outside again, his natural habitat.

In the morning, to my great relief, he was on a chair in the dining-room. The vet came again in the afternoon and gave him another injection and said he was much better, which he obviously was. The next day he gave him the final injection, and by then, the third day, he had already begun to put on a little weight. He was still coughing occasionally, a high-pitched squeaky cough. On the fourth day I gave him tinned food and all was well, but the next day he was sick again, and I wondered whether it was the tinned food or the streptomycin tablets I was giving him, under the vet's instructions. On the sixth day I gave him some of his favourite food, chicken, from one I had roasted for the week-end. It came straight back, and with it so much blood I thought he had haemorrhaged. Greatly alarmed I ran across the road to the vet's house and found him busy in his garden. I apologized for disturbing him at the week-end but begged him to come, telling him about the blood. He said he had none of his equipment at the house, but he would ring his surgery and his colleague who was on duty there would come.

The colleague duly came, a pleasant young man, but Sammy would have none of him, though he did nothing to him that the other vet had not done several times and which had not produced the slightest reaction. I could only conclude that the colleague had not the same 'hands' for a cat. Whatever the reason, Sammy hissed, growled, struggled, clawed. The young man took it all in good part.

'I suppose he just doesn't like me,' he said, amiably.

We discussed the cat, and I said, concerning his bouts of absenteeism, 'It seems so strange that a neutered cat would go off like that!'

The young man asked, 'Why do you call him a neutered cat?'

I replied, puzzled, 'Because I had him neutered!'

The young man smiled, indulgently, humouring a foolish woman.

'This is a full cat,' he said, gently but firmly.

'What do you mean?' I demanded. 'When I got him

64

My little granddaughter, Catherine, loved him from the word go

Tea on the loggia . . . Sammy sharing the sandwiches

Sammy is a cat of character

'Someone outside the law' . . .
the essentially wild creature

three years ago I sent him to a reputable vet for neutering. He was kept there for several days, and when I telephoned to inquire about him was told he had had his operation and was ready to come home. If he wasn't neutered what do you suggest was done to him whilst he was there?'

'Nothing,' he said, simply, and added, 'This cat is entire.'

'Obviously he hasn't been castrated,' I said, 'but *something* must have been done—'

'If he's not castrated he's not neutered.'

'Then what? I mean, a reputable vet doesn't keep a cat for days and return him with nothing done and in due course send in an account for an operation he never had!'

The young man shrugged.

'He could have been overlooked, I suppose. I can only say he's entire.'

I was so shattered by this that I forgot to ask what he considered had caused the haemorrhaging – if it was that.

But though that wasn't explained his absenteeism was. He had spent best part of a week at a vet's, but had escaped the-fate-worse-than-death!

There was, I suddenly discovered, something really rather splendid about it. He was a full cat, not a eunuch. It was sad for him that he had been transplanted to this middle-class district where such female cats as there are have been spayed; but cats doomed to be spayed are often allowed one litter first, and who knew how many such litters he had sired already in all that absenteeism?

The woman in the local bookshop, who is a 'cat' person, and to whom I recounted this extraordinary tale, took an unexpected line; instead of being impressed she was incensed . . . and not against the delinquent vet but against poor Sammy.

'He's probably the father of half my cat's kittens!' she declared, bitterly. 'There are always ginger ones!'

I asked, 'Where do you live?'

She told me and I smiled, happily.

'It wouldn't be too far,' I said, 'for the good news of a queen in season to travel down the wind. It would seem fitting, too, don't you think, that an author's tomcat should mate with a bookseller's queen?'

Her smile was small and thin; unamused.

'I'll let you know when the paperback you want is in,' she said, frigidly.

There's no live-and-let-live with some people. I was elate; not a doubt of it.

'This is a full cat!'

How splendid, how noble a pronouncement!

Chapter Nine

IN deciding that Sammy must be neutered before being brought to me I was bending principle to expediency, for in principle I am opposed to the desexing of animals to suit our convenience; ethically it seems most monstrous; practically it seems, very often, most necessary. The discovery that Sammy had not, in fact, had the monstrous thing done to him, came as a kind of reprieve – I could throw off guilt, for I had been saved from sinning against the light. Hence the euphoria; but behind the euphoria there was also indignation. I had been fooled; all that explaining-away I had done to friends, and to myself. I wrote to the vet who had had Sammy for neutering, asking him if he would agree that only castration would neuter an animal; I had become involved in an argument, I said.

He replied, breezily, yes, only castration; if there was any other method he hadn't heard of it. What discussions I did become involved in! How was the Ilford tiger?

I wrote, sternly: 'Since you acknowledge that only castration neuters an animal, what did you do to the male cat I sent to you three years ago for neutering, and which was kept for several days at your place and then returned to me as fully equipped as he had gone to you?' I added that having eyes in my head, and knowing the facts of life, I could of course see that the cat had not been castrated, but assumed that something else had been done to neuter him, since I in due course received an account for that operation.

In reply he was pleased to be facetious; no doubt, he wrote, under the general anaesthetic, the surgeon in charge had thoroughly groomed the cat's coat and cleaned out his ears, but inadvertently overlooked the major object of the exercise . . .

I answered that I was not amused, and that had I been in his position I would have expressed dismay and concern, and either refunded the fee or offered to do the operation forthwith – to which I would have replied that I appreciated the gesture but would prefer now to leave the cat as he is. I added that so far as I was concerned the matter was closed. I hoped it was, but a few days later I had another letter asking if I was sure that the 'content of the scrotal sac is not organised blood-clot or indurated scar tissue,' declaring this to be 'very possible', and suggesting that an independent professional opinion – for which he was prepared to pay – would be of value. I replied that I had already had *two* professional opinions, from the qualified veterinary surgeons who had recently attended the cat, both of whom had said that the cat was entire and had been puzzled that I should think otherwise. I gave him the name of the young vet and his associates and suggested he should ring the firm – he need not, I said, disclose his name, since I had not done so, but told them only that three years ago I had sent the cat to a reputable vet for neutering. This did conclude the correspondence. I later learned that he did not follow up my suggestion.

Whilst this correspondence was going on Sammy continued to cough and to be unable to keep down food, except for lightly boiled egg and chicken essence. There had been the brief return to tinned food, then the blood, followed by the renewed vomiting. The vet said that his chest condition had cleared up but that the infection had now spread to the throat, and this would account for the vomiting, the food coming straight back, never reaching his stomach. This went on for a week, and then on the Saturday, exactly a week after he had brought up so much blood, he was violently sick bringing up not only what had just gone down but food from the stomach, and cleaning up the mess with an inadequate sheet of newspaper – it was the time of the newspaper strike, and the supply of old newsprint was almost used up – my fingers came in contact with something hard. For a moment I was dismayed thinking I must have left a piece of shell in the breakfast egg; then I realized that this wasn't shell; it was bone; a large V-shaped piece of chicken bone; a piece from the carcass at the first rib, broken off with an inch or more of the rib attached to it; there was a little blood on it.

This, then, was why he had been unable to keep food down; he had had this large bone in his gullet for two weeks to my knowledge, and probably for a week before that. I wondered if the bone had caused the pneumonia, but the vet said no; he couldn't help feeling, he said, that the bone was a red herring . . . I knew what he meant, but it seemed an odd way of putting it. 'Red herring' or not, after Sammy was delivered of the bone he was perfectly all right. How he came by the bone must remain a mystery; he could have picked it up, somewhere, I suppose, though he is not a dustbin cat; he had 'shared a chicken meal', I was told, and he could have been given a bone inadvertently. Only Sammy knows, and Sammy's lips are sealed.

Soon after that I became ill myself and spent most of the week in bed, which was anyhow nice for Sammy, who stayed there with me all day. I do not delude myself that he stayed there out of affection for me, knowing I was unwell; he often stays on the bed all day, and having the missus there for company was a bonus. But come dusk, being a cat, he was off out.

Chapter Ten

BEFORE we leave this subject of neutering I should like to say something about the spaying of cats. How it is with bitches I do not know, but the vet who spayed Lucy many years ago, following the birth of the monster kitten and the development of a septic uterus, I am told now refuses to do the operation. This doesn't surprise me, because after the spaying Lucy developed severe eczema all over her body; it would clear up only to recur some months later. It recurred less frequently as she got older, and less severely, but it did recur. The vet told me that it was due to the spaying; the hormones, he said, with no natural outlet, the cat no longer coming into season, escaped through the skin. He had recommended spaying because with her uterus condition her next pregnancy was likely to be extra-uterus, which could cause her death. This eczema did not always occur in spayed cats, he said, but he had known other cases. I also have known cases, and of people refusing to have their queens spayed for that reason. I have also known spayed cats who have not – I have been assured by their owners – suffered in this way.

I was for a long time deeply opposed to the neutering of female cats; it seemed to me a quite horrible thing to do; nevertheless, when the vet recommended that Lucy be spayed I accepted his recommendation not only in the cat's interests but in my own, for a female cat in season presents problems, and I was by then already beginning to weary of them. It is not only the problem of how to dispose of the kittens – which can be as many as five at a time – and of using up all the friends and acquaintances who are prepared to take a kitten; there is also the problem of the males spraying around the premises. I have met cat-lovers who have assured me they do not mind this smell; to me it is a quite indescribably dreadful smell, and when, as sometimes happened, the toms got into the house and left their visiting cards I would feel quite hysterical.

Lucy, as I have said, used to come up over a low roof and through a window into a small room she inhabited when I was away; this room was always spring-cleaned on my return and Lucy no longer used it, but there must have been some smell of her left in it, nevertheless, for the toms found their way to it. They came, also, into other rooms if windows or doors were left open, and when they could not get into the rooms they sprayed the outsides of the doors and windows. The vet who spayed Lucy told me that the liquid discharged when the toms back up against something to spray is from a gland near the anus; it is not urine, as is commonly supposed. Its function is to attract the female, whereas in the skunk the evil-smelling liquid squirted from the anal glands, for a distance of some eight or twelve feet, is a weapon of defence and this activity is not confined to the male; the skunk, though somewhat like a cat in appearance and build, is not of the cat tribe. The big cats spray, and I once saw a lion back up to the bars of its cage and do so, the shower catching some of the humans who stared at him.

I became so neurotic about the toms spraying around the house, and sometimes in the house, when Lucy was in season, that I admit to being relieved when the vet declared that in her case it was a spayed cat or a dead cat; whether I should eventually have had her done otherwise I don't know, but probably – offering up the feeling of guilt as a sop to conscience. I have always admired people who have resolutely kept their female cats entire and coped with the succession of litters – and the card-leaving toms. My daughter never had her Mitzi-cat spayed, and this cat came into season almost to the end of her twenty-one years of life. Towards the end she would give birth to only one kitten – or none.

Michael Joseph was another who raised all the kittens God sent – it quite simply could not have occurred to him to do anything else. In his book, *Cat's Company,** he does not even discuss any possible alternative. At one time, he tells us, he disposed of kittens to the animal department of a big stores and found they would take all he could supply, though they did after a time request more 'gentleman' kittens than 'ladies'. He had not thought about payment, and was astonished when he eventually received a cheque – addressed to him as Michael Joseph, Esq., Cat-breeder. The kittens from the litters of his famous and beloved cat, Minna-Minna-Mowbray, were in such demand from friends and acquaintances that the demand exceeded the supply.

The danger of supplying kittens – or puppies – to animal departments or pet stores is that they can be bought up by people who resell them to laboratories for vivisection. There is no protection from this iniquitous trade except by making vivisection illegal – which I am personally strongly in favour of. Even if it furthers the cause of science in the interests of Man, have we the *right* to use animals in this way?

* 1930, revised edition 1946, reprinted 1970.

I was delighted when I learned in 1969 that the firm founded by Michael Joseph was publishing an anti-vivisection book by my friend John Vyvyan, the Shakespearean scholar, *In Pity and in Anger, a Study of the use of Animals in Science*. Michael had been dead some years by then, but certainly he would have approved, for although cats were his first love, and had been since boyhood, he also had affection for dogs, and he would have been appalled, had he lived, to learn of the trade in cats and dogs specially bred in this country for medical research and exported to Japan, where anaesthetics are not regarded as necessary for experiments carried out on living animals.

A strong case can be made out for the neutering of domestic pets in this context. Can we be sure that all the pretty little kittens and puppies we see in the pet stores, and in the pets departments of big stores, are all really going to good homes – or, for that matter, to homes at all? It is so easy to take a litter along, feeling virtuous about not having the little creatures destroyed, but we cannot be sure of the good homes, and we can be sure of the existence of the laboratories in which medical research is carried out on living animals, and where the demand for these victims of science exceeds supply. In this context it does seem better to keep down the animal population – which can only be done by castrating the males and spaying the females.

A case can also be made out in the case of male cats that neutering spares them the torment of sexual frustration in a society in which the chances of an entire male meeting an unspayed female are increasingly remote (dogs would appear to have even less chance of a sex life, since most owners of bitches keep them in when on heat). This had been in my mind when I decided that Sammy would be better neutered; not only would he more readily settle down in his new environment, I thought, but also he would be spared the frustration a full male cat must experience in a district in which there were very few cats of either sex, and such females as there were undoubtedly spayed.

In his Ilford days, his former owner told me, he had had a girl-friend, a pretty little striped cat who sometimes came home with him, but whom he never allowed to eat from his plate. When I had believed him to be neutered I had often thought with regret of his girl-friend; now that I know he is a full cat I still think of her with regret, wishing that she, or her counterpart, was around here. If such a little unspayed female was available he would joyfully beget kittens on her, which would be nice for them both, but would it really be such a good thing? Where would those litters end up? Our world being what it so abominably is perhaps it is more humane to do the expedient thing than the principled thing? *Can* what is wrong in principle ever be right in practice? But then again, it seems to me, we have to define our principles. Are we postulating the principle of preserving the natural law inviolate? Or are we concerned with the principle of minimising cruelty to animals?

For and against neutering the case would appear to be more heavily weighted on the side of neutering – which for me means the assertion of the intellect and the recoil of instinct and emotion. I am too old, now, for Sammy to have any successors, but I think that if I had a female cat now I would not have her spayed but would have all but one, or at most two, of her litter destroyed before their eyes were open – in fact almost immediately. With Lucy's kittens I always tried to keep the males in the litter – it is quite easy to sex newborn kittens – because males are easier to 'place'. I do not, honestly, think she missed those that were taken away from her when her back was turned; she appeared always to settle down contentedly enough with what was left, even when it was only one.

It was a great grief to me as a child that my grandmother, on the farm, invariably drowned all of her house-cat's kittens, after which the bereaved mother would wander all over the house crying pitifully, looking for them. It seemed to me most terribly cruel – and it is.

Lafcadio Hearn, who had a very great love for cats, tells a moving story about one of his cats, Tama, in his book, *Kotto*. She was a Japanese cat, for Hearn lived the last years of his life in Japan; Tama had one litter very happily, but was unfortunate in her second pregnancy, returning one evening after a visit to a street some distance away 'hurt by some brutal person', and her kittens were born dead. It seemed that she also might die, but she recovered, though remained 'troubled in spirit by the loss of her kittens'. She could not understand that they were dead, and went everywhere in the house looking for them, long after they had been buried in the garden. Her owner had to open all the drawers and cupboards in the house, over and over again, he says, to prove to her that her kittens were not there. She knew she had given birth, and that therefore there ought to be kittens. Finally she was able to convince herself that the kittens were not in the house and that it was useless to look for them any more. They became dream kittens. 'She plays with them in dreams,' Lafcadio Hearn wrote, 'and coos to them, and catches for them small shadowy things – perhaps even brings to them, through some dim window of memory, a sandal or ghostly straw . . .'

Tama was lucky to have Lafcadio Hearn as her owner,

for the Japanese lack of imagination where animals are concerned is total, as I have seen for myself when I journeyed throughout Japan. I was once given a book about a cat by a Japanese friend; it was called *I am a cat*, and was by a Japanese writer. It was given to me 'because you are a cat lover'. Apart from being an extremely silly book, by any standard, it ends with a cat swimming round in a barrel of water, unable to climb out . . .

When I was staying at this man's house, outside Tokyo, he asked me once, handing me my mail, from whom it was I had so many letters. I told him from the friend in London who went to my house to feed my cat. He gazed at me in amazement for a long moment, then said, very slowly, 'To *feed* . . . your *cat*?'

Perhaps there is after all something in the extra sensory perception of cats, for when, recently, being in England, this Japanese friend stayed at my house, Sammy was about to get up into his lap, because he always does get into the lap of anyone who sits in that particular armchair; but having stood up on his hindlegs, with his forepaws on an arm of the chair, he looked into the face of the man who sat there . . . then changed his mind, dropped down on to all fours, and walked away.

Chapter Eleven

IN the autumn of 1966, shortly after Lucy had died, I saw
Derek Tangye's new book, *Lama*, in a shop window. I
bought it because the black cat depicted on the jacket
reminded me so strongly of Lucy. The book interested me
a good deal; it recounts the patient efforts to induce a small
half-wild black cat – Lama – to come and live-in, and how
eventually she was the cat that came in from the storm. I
could not know that a few months later I would be similarly
coaxing a cat to make its home with me. When, after
Christmas, I was similarly putting down saucers that were
sometimes emptied and sometimes not, and similarly
glimpsing a cat that always refused to have anything to do
with me, I wrote to the author of *Lama* and told him I had
bought the book because Lama looked so like Lucy, and of
Lucy's death and my resolve not to have another cat, but
how I had fallen for a honey-coloured cat in need of a home,
but who rejected the home I offered him, and of my
watching and waiting and my despair. He replied very
sympathetically, urging me not to reproach myself over
Lucy, and confident that I would eventually succeed with
the new cat as he and his wife, Jeannie, had with Lama, and
later with a black kitten – offspring of the elusive grey cat
they became convinced was Lama's mother – they similarly
coaxed.

It was a very encouraging letter, as were other letters
commenting on my 'progress reports', and I re-read the

passages in the book about the saucers and the watching and waiting, the hoping and despairing and the bouts of wondering why they bothered.

It was a great day when at last I was able to send Derek Tangye photographs of the cat I had worked so hard to get – photographs taken in the house. He sent me warm congratulations. But why, really, *does* one bother – and to the point of obsession? In India you work very hard for your tiger, either to shoot it or photograph it, for the excitement of it; but when it comes to this very little tiger, the domestic cat – why then the watching and the waiting, the patience, the stubborn determination to succeed?

But is there ever any logical explanation of an obsession? Something takes hold of the imagination and possesses it. We say that someone has a 'thing' about something. Some of us have a 'thing' about cats. They arouse our imaginative sympathy, our compassion, and our possessiveness. We care about them, we worry about them, we love them, and persuade ourselves they love us – but there, I think, we are mistaken. They sit in our laps because they like the warmth of our bodies; when we have been away and return they are pleased to see us, weaving round our legs and rubbing themselves against us and purring madly, not, I think, from affection but because we represent security, food, the guarantee of their well-being; and because they like company. I know that many distinguished cat-lovers, of all nationalities and all through history, have thought otherwise; presumptuous as it may seem on my part, I think they flattered themselves. Cats like human company, but that is another matter. When I am out all day, if I leave Sammy on my bed he is invariably there when I get back late in the evening; if I am here, though he may stay on the bed for some hours after I have left it, suddenly he will join me in the study. When I am gardening he will leave a comfortable cushioned garden seat and come marching down a path to where I am working, as though to see what I am doing. When I am on my knees, grubbing in the earth, he will sit beside me and watch; when I move on he moves on – until we come to the catmint, and then he usually stops – to pounce on it, chew a stem, roll in it, and if I attempt to stroke him then he will as likely as not dab out at me, spitefully. Catmint seems to have an extraordinary effect on cats; I have heard it suggested that it is aphrodisiac, but I have never come to any conclusions about it; in my observation it seems to go straight to their heads, as though it were some kind of powerful cat cocktail. Possibly, also, it is medicinally good for them, as is grass, though a cat does not eat grass as a cow or a horse does, but chews the stalks, and I have watched both Lucy and Sammy searching for grass stalks, ignoring just grass in terms of blades. I have also observed that cats do not chew grass stalks or catmint regularly, which suggests that both have medicinal properties and are to be taken as required. Sometimes, even when I have shaken the clump of catmint, to release the pungent scent, Sammy has remained uninterested; at other times he rolls over at the first whiff of it.

This is a very good garden for cats – as it is for children – because it is on different levels and has numerous hide-outs in shrubberies and a bit of woodland. For a cat it is a miniature jungle; Lucy made it her private jungle; Sammy stalks it with a proprietorial air like the very-little-tiger that he is. In the hot weather he 'lies up' in it, as the tiger lies up in the Indian jungles waiting for sundown. Like the tiger he does not lie up in any old shady corner, but chooses a

Sammy playing at being a pretty pussy

'So Tiberius would have sat,
Had Tiberius been a cat' . . .

Throughout history most writers have liked cats
(*Photograph of the Author and Sammy by Paul Tanqueray*)

strategic position in which no enemy can surprise him, and from which he can see what is going on; like the tiger, therefore, he favours high ground for his siesta. There is a bank covered with St John's Wort he likes; lying in there, hidden by the bushy little plants, between a lilac tree and a tall lombardy-poplar flowering cherry, the imprint of his body there, day after day, for weeks on end, makes an oblong 'nest', to which he regularly returns for the duration – that is to say, for as long as he is using this particular site.

What decides a cat that a favourite spot is favourite no more? There is no means of knowing, and part of the fascination of cats is their mysteriousness and their unpredictability. When Sammy has had enough of the St John's Wort bank he goes up the slope to the rhododendrons – not to lie in their deep cool shade, but in a semi-open place at a point where the bushes come down to meet a large azalea above some steps. From here he can look out one way down to the loggia and the house, and across the pond to the St John's Wort, and the other way he covers the slope; it is, in fact, a good look-out post. He has had several nests here among the dry dead leaves, and his tawny coat becomes protective colouring. It is, in fact, quite hard to see him when he gets in among the dead leaves, so perfectly does he blend with them. There is no scooping out to make a nest; he simply selects the precise spot where he wishes to settle down and the instant pressure of his body does the rest.

By the same process he has fashioned a tunnel through a thicket of elm tree brushwood into the drive of the house that lies back behind here. I discovered this once, when searching for him during one of his spells of absenteeism.

Simply by passing through the undergrowth repeatedly he has worn it completely smooth, rounding it to the width of his body. I was led to it first by following his imprints in the snow; then one day I was able to follow him; when he emerged into the drive he looked at me, angrily, and said, very plainly, 'Stop it! Go away!' I went away but watched over the fence from farther up; I had to know where he went. He crossed the drive, jumped a kind of embankment wall, and from there sprang to the top of a wooden fence above it, then dropped down into the garden of a corner house. From there he could, if he chose, by jumping walls and fences, or finding a way through or round them traverse the entire length of the road without leaving the gardens. Perhaps he does; I shall never know; and strictly, I suppose, it is not my business.

When he leaves this garden his business is the endless search for a female – 'always seeking and seldom finding', as Hemingway said – in *The Old Man and the Sea* – about the gulls endlessly circling over their sea in their search for food. I had hoped to spare him all that, but if I had succeeded in that well-meaning intention what would have been the point of his existence? It brings us back to the question of neutering, the case for and against, and with such valid arguments on both sides I find myself quite unable to take a stand. I only know that, irrationally, perhaps – even sentimentally, if you like – I am glad that Sammy is after all a full cat.

The contented owners of contented eunuchs will have no patience with such an attitude, I know, and they could be right. But in writing about the mixed-up cat that was Sammy I cannot avoid writing also about his mixed-up owner that is me.

Chapter Twelve

M OST children are fond of cats, but most, if not all, cats are far from fond of strange children – that is to say, children with whom they have not grown up and whom they have not learned to tolerate. Lucy, who never had anything to do with children, was terrified of them, and a child with its sudden movements, eager voice, fluttering hands, had only to come into a room for her to dive for shelter or rush wildly out. Sammy, who was reared amongst children, was, as I have said, very good-natured with them, but his former owner told me that he 'never liked strange children', and this was evident when he first met Catherine, then only about six years old, and it has taken him a long time to become accustomed to her – it was over three years before he would sit on her lap. Even now he is not quite sure that he accepts her, and there are times when he will not take food from her.

It is, I think, the eager reaching hands of children they don't know, or don't know well, that cats mistrust. In general I would think puppies are easier for children than cats, since they are always willing to play and are not nervous. Cats are essentially nervous creatures – Dr Méry goes further and says neurotic! – by which I don't mean timid, for they are not that, but, on the contrary, extremely courageous, but creatures of a highly developed nervous system. A cat, once it has passed kittenhood, is not always willing either to play or to accept caresses and attention;

sometimes it quite simply wants to be left alone – to get on with its endless washing, or its even more endless sleeping . . . neither of which does a young child understand. A dog is a much more amiable and accommodating creature. A cat can be amiable if it feels like it, a pretty purring pussy inviting attention and responding to it; then suddenly it will decide it has had enough and will jump down from a lap and stalk away as though it had suddenly remembered something important, or, hurtfully, will go off and make itself comfortable somewhere else. An adult understands such feline behaviour; the child does not, and probably pursues the cat, who, impatiently, dabs out. Sammy is now fairly reliable with Catherine, even when she 'pesters' him with her love; with Lucy she would have had no chance at all.

Long before Catherine, and long before a ginger tom pounced on Sammy's mother and added a honey-coloured son to her litter, during the reign of Lucy, there was a child in the house below this one – a small boy with a rather pathetic look and sticking-out ears and a shy smile; he was the owner of a very handsome young striped male cat he called Frisky, and of whom he was obviously fond. I would watch him carrying the cat round the garden, and lying face downwards on the grass playing with it, dangling a bit of string with a twist of paper tied at the end. They made a charming pair, the pale young boy with his dark hair, the grey young cat with his dark stripes, and something somehow wistful about them both.

Often when the boy was away the cat would come over the fence, and from the safe vantage point of half-way up a cherry-tree scour the landscape, hopefully. Lucy always seemed to know when he was there – the tom-cat smell, I suppose, went down the wind – and before I had spotted Frisky in the cherry-tree I would know he was there, by the way she lifted her head and the direction in which she gazed, though from where she sat he would not be visible to her. Presently she would get up, leisurely, mount some steps to a higher level of the garden, stroll, daintily, a short distance along a path, and then, when he was in view, sit down and look at him – coolly. The long cool look that cats are so good at. He would look back at her, not coolly, but intently – almost hypnotically, as though he tried to will her into submission.

At first he was nervous of approaching her; she was not in season, and, though he did not know it, never likely to be, but she was female, and hope springs eternal. She did not repel him, and as time went on he became bolder and descended from the cherry-tree to the border below, venturing to within a few yards of her – whilst she would sit in the middle of the path handing out that long cool look. It was interesting, and a little amusing – and sad. Not divine but human intervention came between them. I would feel guilty.

Once, daringly, when Lucy was in the room above, he took the flying leap on to the low roof and stayed there, calling to her: *My Love! My Love! My Love! Come out! Come out! Come out!* But Lucy did not even bother to go to the window to say Hullo, or Go away. He never dared to scramble up the roof-tiles and into the room, any more than in the garden he ever dared to come close to her. She, for her part, would regard him with that mild interest, neither repelling nor actively inviting. It was as though at that time, soon after she was spayed, she still had hormones enough left to have an eye for an attractive male . . . though later she would chase any interloper off the premises in a fury.

Disloyally, I always thought how much more beautiful was the young Frisky-cat, with his fine markings, than half-Persian Lucy – who was not even a good black, really, but prune-coloured. When I brought her to London from Devon I brought also a ginger kitten from the same litter, a lively little chap, whom I'd much rather have had, but he was booked to go to a friend of my daughter's; it was only Lucy, the devil-cat, whose life was threatened – the unwanted female. I brought them by train, in a large basket, which was left in the guard's van; the ginger kitten made a lot of noisy fuss – 'Let me out! Let me out!' – but his sister merely philosophically slept.

I had both kittens here for a few days, and then little Ginger was collected by his new owner, and I was left with Lucy – after craftily suggesting to the friend that the female kitten was really prettier, and she could have her if she liked – I really didn't mind which I had. But the friend said she wanted a tom, and she liked ginger cats . . .

The family with the little boy who owned Frisky moved away – they had been there only temporarily, anyhow, the house having been requisitioned during the War. Other cats came and went in the garden – always males, in their endless search, drawn by the scent of the female . . . but never a tiger cat. Where were all the ginger cats gone? Were they a dying breed? Before the advent of Sammy there had been only little Ginger, in transit. That very-little-tiger was not 'meant', but Sammy was destined to become part of my life from the moment I first set eyes on him, when he was no bigger than Lucy's little brother had been in that brief encounter.

86

But I never regretted dusky Lucy; she was decorative around the place, and her litters were fun until they became too much; I came to accept her indifference as an expression of that feline independence one heard so much about, and became fond of her. I wrote a novella about her, which I called *So Tiberius*,* taking the title from the Matthew Arnold poem; it was about a man and a cat in their relationships with the opposite sex, their lives in this respect running parallel, but the cat made a better job of life, having no emotional involvements.

I felt affection for Lucy, but not until the pitifulness of the end did she deeply engage my emotions, whereas Sammy, the Ilford tiger, the little feller, did so from the start.

Sammy is a cat of character, and we have established a degree of communication. He has come to understand certain inflections of my voice, and I have come to understand various observations of his. We get along, really, remarkably well; occasionally we bicker a bit, and tell each other off, but for the most part I feel affection for him, and he demonstrates liking for me – and more than that I don't think a human being should expect from a cat; to get that much is a good deal. I don't think we should attempt to endow animals with human emotions. Dogs, perhaps; I don't know much about dogs, but they seem to establish a higher degree of communication with humans than cats do, and certainly they fret after their owners when parted from them, which I do not think is the case with cats – though I am sure many cat-lovers will strongly disagree with me.

I am not a 'dog person', and I am a 'cat person', but all the same I do not think a cat is companionable in the way

* 1954

that a dog manifestly is; a creature that during the day is mostly asleep and during the night mostly out cannot be said to be much in the way of company. Lucy was mostly in at nights, on the chair beside me as I worked, but she was also mostly asleep.

It is quite irrational to have a 'thing' about cats, but there it is, some of us have it, and we can take refuge for our foolishness – if it is that – in the fact that very many distinguished and highly intelligent people have had it down through the ages.

It is all part of the mystery and magic of the Cat.

I like very much a frivolous, but nevertheless percipient, little book entitled, *How to Live with a Calculating Cat*.* William Nettleton, who wrote the text for Eric Gurney's drawings, evidently knows cats, and a book like this, with humour glossing some shrewd observation, can tell one more about cats than all the 'scholarly treatises, incredibly comprehensive', which would 'simply cause any well-adjusted cat to snicker behind his whiskers'. I like particularly the observation that the 'really great thing about cats is their endless variety. One can pick a cat to fit almost any kind of décor, colour scheme, income, personality, mood, that sort of thing. But under the fur, whatever colour it may be, there still lies, essentially unchanged, *one of the world's free souls*'.

The italics are mine; I think those words contain the clue to the fascination the cat has for humans, who believe in freedom, and fight for it, and even die for it, but seldom, if ever achieve it.

* First published, 1962. New English Library Edition, 1968.

Chapter Thirteen

SINCE his eight-day absence in the summer, and the subsequent illness, Sammy has not been away; we have got through the tangy days of autumn and are now well into November, but there have been no frosts, no sting in the air, nothing to set a cat's whiskers tingling and his blood stirring. There have been, as yet, no other cats around; all is quiet in this small jungle. Only the squirrels, scuttling about harvesting acorns and chestnuts, and helping themselves to bread put out for the birds – and to any crocus bulbs they can get at – insist that winter is closing in. Some of the squirrels are young and very small, no bigger than average-sized rats, and one of these days, I suppose, a youngling will linger too long grubbing in the drifts of dead leaves, and Sammy, camouflaged the same colour as the leaves, will pounce. Well, they are a pest in the garden, these 'tree-rats', but next time Sammy makes a kill I hope he will not bring it into the house, or eat it outside the back door whilst I am having my lunch in the kitchen . . . impelling me to look, knowing I won't like what I see.

Lucy, in her youth, brought innumerable birds into the house – usually dead, but sometimes not; those that were not I could make her give up, and when they had recovered from the shock of their experience they would fly off – to my intense relief. Occasionally she would bring a field-mouse into the house and put it down alive, then have a great time chasing it around the room – to the intense annoyance of my late husband, Reginald Reynolds, who was a vegetarian and a pacifist, and whose services would be enlisted for rescuing the poor little thing. He was not a cat person, nor, particularly, a dog person. He was not an 'animal lover', but defended their right to live. Concerning animals as domestic pets he was neutral, though inclining to my mother's view that you were better without them. In the early 'thirties, before I knew him, he inherited a mongrel dog he called Lenin, of whom he became quite fond, but with whom he felt forced to part when he found that the dog, unlike its namesake, was not allowed into the British Museum. He would conscientiously look after Lucy during my absences in Ireland, but being himself a strict vegetarian regarded with distaste the fish and rabbit he found himself required to ladle out to her. He had some vegetarian friends, it seems, who had brought their cat up to subsist on porridge . . .

I think he might have taken to Sammy, though – so long as he didn't see him dealing with a squirrel. He would have recognized him as a 'character'; he had immense sympathy, too, for the pushed-around, the displaced and dispossessed, the maladjusted, and Sammy when he first came here was all of that. He would have liked the little feller just because he was that – the *little* feller, common or garden, *gamin*, with a Cockney perkiness and pluckiness and resilience.

Tim, who is devoted to Sammy, but who nevertheless prefers cats to be Siamese, sometimes tells him, to keep him in his place, 'You are a very *ordinary* cat! There are a great many cats just like you!'

But, as I point out to him, that isn't quite true; Sammy is not just a ginger tom; he is ginger only on the top of his back; the rest of him is pure honey; his head is blonde; and he is unique in the black freckles in his mouth and on his little pink nose.

The first day he was here, that upsetting day when he cried and cried, and prowled and prowled, when, exhausted, he finally slept for a while, I thought how well he toned with the room – with the books, the faded Indian divan cover, the faded orange curtains; he 'blended' . . . which prune-coloured Lucy never did. He blends in the summer, too, with the roses in the garden, and in the autumn with the dead leaves, and the gold and copper of the azaleas.

He is very beautiful. Not in the subtle, elegant Siamese fashion, but in the way that the Great Cats of the jungles are beautiful; a wild-animal beauty, a little harsh.

He is not shy. Lucy always fled when people came to the house; this cat regards them with mild interest. If advances are made to him he does not always respond, but he bears with it. Occasionally he does the visitor the honour of getting into his or her lap. Fortunately most of the people who come here are people who like cats. But once there was a woman who was appalled, shrinking back in her chair.

'He won't hurt you,' I said. Then, what should have occurred to me in the first place, 'But perhaps you don't like cats?'

'I don't *mind* cats,' she said, 'but this is such a *big* cat!'

'First-cousin to a tiger,' I assured her, and removed him.

Once, too, he climbed up on to the crossed knees of a man who dislikes cats. He could not get comfortable at all on those high-perched knees, and the owner of the knees did not intend that he should.

I watched, maliciously, wondering who would give in. Cats can be very tenacious. But after a minute or two

Sammy jumped down from the uncomfortable pyramid; there were, after all, more accommodating laps in the room.

It is interesting to watch the reaction of a person who is 'neutral' about animals when a cat gets into the lap that neither welcomes nor denies. The neutralist regards the creature with a small indulgent smile – the smile of reluctant toleration. Reluctant because, of course, the neutralist doesn't really like cats. As an Irishwoman said to me during the War, 'Sure, we're neutral, but who are we neutral against?' The neutral lap does not refuse, but also it does not accommodate, and no self-respecting cat wastes much time on it.

At first Sammy was very promiscuous in the matter of laps. Latterly he has given up the habit of jumping into the lap of anyone who sits in a certain armchair, and if it's not Tim sitting there he is not interested. A curious habit is that before jumping on to Tim's knees he first sharpens his claws on the side of the chair. Occasionally he goes over to the armchair, sharpens his claws and then after all doesn't jump up. Why he has to sharpen his claws on the furniture when there are so many trees outside will always remain a mystery. He does use the trees, but it doesn't prevent him from shredding the upholstery, but like all other cat people I never utter more than a mild protest. I have read some-where that this claw-sharpening is not in fact that but claw-cleaning; though about this I wonder. So many theories are advanced about cats, I think, because we know, really, so little about them.

Chapter Fourteen

WHATEVER is true or not true in much that is claimed for cats, one thing is certain, and that is their quite astonishing sense of hearing, though Dr Méry says that remarkable as it is it is slightly inferior to that of dogs. 'The cat's ear,' he says, 'is receptive to frequencies of from 20 to 25,000 vibrations per second,' whereas the dogs is sensitive up to 35,000. Even in sleep cats are alert, he says, to the slightest tremor that they alone can perceive.

This I have observed in Sammy. He will be curled up tightly and to all appearances sunk in a deep sleep, though I sit typing beside him, and go in and out of the room making no attempt to open and close the door quietly; none of this impinges on his sleep; but if someone comes up the stairs, perhaps so softly that I, typing, do not hear, his eyes open, his ears prick forward. The click of the typewriter, the opening and closing of the door, are familiar sounds, fusing into the background of his sleep, but the step on the stair – that is something different, unfamiliar and therefore commanding alertness. It impinges, and he is awake; if someone familiar comes into the room he closes his eyes again, relaxes, sinks back into sleep; but if it is the man about the telephone, a total stranger, he not merely surfaces from asleep but is very wide awake indeed.

The only time I have seen him terrified and diving for shelter was when a workman entered the kitchen in which he was sleeping on a chair and, preparatory to doing a job, took off his jacket and hung it over the back of that chair. I have no idea what significance this had for Sammy but he leapt from the chair and dived under the table. At the time I thought perhaps it was associated with his experience at the vet's, not knowing then, of course, that really nothing very alarming had happened to him there . . . though, I suppose, the whole experience could have been alarming, being shut up in a confined space, in a strange place, amongst strangers. I was told that during those days at the vet's he lay up on the shelf provided in the cage, or pen, or whatever they call it, and was 'very reserved' when approached. I have wondered, since, just how much of an understatement that was. Perhaps he took refuge in sleep, or feigned sleep, as an escape from it all.

His acute cat's hearing can be disturbing. Sometimes, after dark, in the winter, when he is still in here with me in the study, and all is peaceful, the curtains closed, the gas-fire softly hissing, the sounds of cars muted, tea and the six o'clock news over, but too early, yet, for him to go out or for me to pour the first drink of the evening, he will suddenly start up, wide awake, tense, listening. Perhaps it is a still night and there is not even the sound of an owl, or the high thin bleep of a bat, but he has heard something out there in the darkness, and turns his head from the small window to the big one, and back again, and I have fantasies of someone lurking out there, moving round the house. Then I, too, am tense, listening . . . though this is foolish, for what he has heard is something ultra-sonic and totally beyond my human range of hearing. It is all the same unnerving, when you sit alone, entirely surrounded by garden and darkness. My daughter, sitting alone in a very much greater solitude, would have the same experience with

Mitzi-cat suddenly starting up, pricking her ears, alert. 'It's like having a little dog!' she would say. 'She makes me quite nervous!'

It can happen in daylight, too. Tea on the loggia on a summer afternoon; Sammy has shared the crab-spread sandwiches and sampled the iced cake and lapped up some top-of-the-milk. The sun shines, the fountain plays, the goldfish glide under the water-lily leaves; there are birds, assorted, and not more than the usual week-end quota of jet 'planes intermittently making conversation impossible; in short, as peaceful a Saturday afternoon as you could reasonably expect in a London suburb towards the end of the twentieth century. The author gently rocks herself in a dilapidated rocking-chair, a woman friend in a deck-chair recounts to her, between 'planes, her impressions of a dress rehearsal of a ballet at Covent Garden, Sammy is stretched out in the sunshine at the top of the loggia steps, as luxuriously relaxed as only a cat knows how. Then suddenly he rolls over, his forepaws firmly planted on the step, his tail lashing.

The friend breaks off her cultural narrative to demand, 'What is it, Sammy?'

The cat ignores the inquiry and sits up, turning his head from right to left.

'He has heard something,' I say, anxiously, and peer towards a large wrought-iron gate that shuts off the main garden from the front of the house, and is designed to prevent callers who knock and get no reply at the front door from walking round – as happened in the bad old days before the gate.

The friend volunteers to investigate.

'If anyone's there I'll say you're not here.'

She mounts the steps from the loggia and goes along to the gate; there's no one there.

'It's all right, Sammy,' she says, resuming her seat and passing her cup.

Sammy is a long way from being convinced; he is now balanced on his hindlegs, his front paws folded against his chest, and looking like nothing so much as a miniature kangaroo. In this absurd posture he turns from right to left, left to right.

I refill the cup and pass it back.

'What on *earth*, Sammy,' I say, a little irritated.

The friend says, 'No use being cross with him – he heard something.'

'He imagines things,' I assert, impatiently.

It is several minutes before Sammy drops down on to all-fours, and even then he is not relaxed, but still alert. I think: he really can be the most ridiculous cat at times; what he probably heard was a field-mouse taking a stroll, or a squirrel stowing away the week-end shopping in its larder in the hollow of a tree. Wild life abounds in the best London suburbs.

When the guest had gone I went as always when alone into the study. There I was dismayed to discover that the watercolour of the Shwedagon Pagoda, Rangoon, which has hung above my mantelpiece since I got back from Burma in 1954, had crashed, taking a little gilded statuette of the goddess Avalokitesvara with it. It was this, then, that Sammy had heard, and which had turned him into a little kangaroo, a sound he did not understand and had not been able to locate.

Gathering up the fragments of broken glass I felt I owed him an apology . . .

There was another occasion in day-time when he knew very well what the sound was that disturbed him, and where it came from, and did his best to tell me, but my human denseness prevented me from understanding. It was a day of high wind, lashing rain, and general misery – the worst kind of English November day. I hate wind – any kind of wind, the hot desert wind, the kamseen, which sweeps into Cairo and burns all the plants on all the balconies brown, the nerve-fraying grey mistral of the south of France, the dusty sirocco, the cold English north-easters, the wet wild south-westerlies, all high winds everywhere. In my Irish days I would feel demented, as the Irish say, by the great west winds sweeping in from the Atlantic. I felt demented that November day when the wind was baying round the house like a pack of ravening wolves, and Sammy was fidgeting, distracting me from the letters I was determined to get away by the five-thirty post.

Then suddenly he sprang up from the chair by my desk and leapt up on to a bookshelf and stood there looking out of the window, his tail lashing. It was a raging inferno of movement outside, the tall elms clashing together at the top of the slope, and from the other windows trees of all kinds swaying and tossing, wildly. But it had been going on all day, and I didn't see the point of Sammy getting excited about it now . . . soon it would be dark and the curtains could be drawn and it could all be shut out.

Sammy looked out of the small window and then back at me.

'Wow!' he said, plaintively. 'Wow-ow-ow!'

'I know,' I said, impatiently. 'It's horrible. *I* hate it too, but there's nothing we can do about it!'

He looked at me, then decided, I suppose, that I was

really very stupid, and jumped down from the bookshelf and sat in the middle of the floor looking huffy.

I went on with the letters and he went on sitting there; it was a kind of protest sit-in. When I got up to take the letters to the post he went on sitting there; when I got back he was on the chair near my desk again, but with his back turned to me. Cats can be great back-turners.

I went over to the window to draw the curtains, and then I saw . . . the storm had brought down a big old laburnum tree, which lay all across the rhododendrons. The rhododendrons had broken its fall, so there had been no crash, but Sammy nevertheless had heard, the cleaving of the air, the groan of the crushed rhododendrons, the whimper of the leaves.

'Sorry, Cat,' I said, as I closed the curtains. 'I didn't understand. I still don't speak the language very well. Let me know if you want to go out, but on a night like this you'd do better to stay in . . . '

But he didn't stay in. The wind subsided a little, later, and there was an almost full moon scudding through the clouds, and it was not all that cold. Not that cats mind nights being cold, or even wet, though in general, I think, they don't like wind. Anyhow Sammy went out, if only, perhaps, to show his contempt for me and my human stupidity.

When, a week or so later, the tree surgeons came to remove the tree Sammy did not mind the dreadful sound of the mechanical saw in the least; at the sound of steps and voices in the garden he instantly looked up from the corner where he was dozing beside the fire, listened for a few moments, then lowered his head again and resumed the dozing which by the time the saw started had become a deep sleep. Cats do not seem to mind noise; what disturbs and alerts them are the noiseless noises which only they hear – the soundless, to the human ear, approach of another cat in the garden, what Dr Méry calls the ultra-sonic sounds. Vesey-FitzGerald is emphatic that cats become accustomed to noise, such as that of a busy city street with heavy traffic, and ignore it. He lived for a time on a very busy London road, he tells us, and had with him an eight-year-old cat that had been born and bred in the country, but he would go out on the pavement in the rush-hours and sit watching the traffic thundering past and being stroked by strangers. He showed no signs of suffering in all the noise and bustle, but went out and about as freely as he had in the country, and when he returned 'set about the local rats and mice as though he had never been away'.

The country has its dangers, too, for cats; my daughter's cat, Mitzi, was twice caught in a steel trap – which evil things are still in use although they have been made illegal. After the second occasion one of Mitzi's paws developed gangrene and the vet said she should be 'put down'; my daughter did not agree and dealt with the gangrene herself; the cat lost a toe, but the gangrene did not spread and Mitzi lived, as I have said, to the great age of twenty-one.

Cats, too, can be run over in narrow country lanes no less than on busy town or suburban roads; in town and country alike they can pick up poison and be stolen for the iniquitous laboratory trade. A cat's life, no less than a human being's, is fraught with danger. But as Vesey-FitzGerald points out, a long life is not necessarily a happy one. Only I would wish, always, that a cat – or a dog, or any animal – should be spared the horror of the vivisection laboratory. Yet if we live always in dread that terrible things may happen to our pets, or ourselves, we spoil life for ourselves and them whilst the going is good.

Before we leave the subject of cats and noise something should perhaps be said about cats and music. There are those who assert that some cats actually like music. Vesey-Fitz-Gerald says that most cats like music of some sort, and cites the case of a cat that loved the sound of the organ in the village church and always went in when it was being played. Dr Méry devotes an entire chapter of his book to The Cat and Music. He says that the cat's senses are too highly developed, 'from its auditory acuteness to the sensitivity of its whiskers, for it not to react to a marked degree to music.' He then asks, 'But to what sort of music?' Music consists of vibrations, and it is impossible for the cat to be indifferent to them; but does this natural reaction add up to liking? Dr Méry cites examples of cats who are said by their owners to have found pleasure in the sound of music of one kind or another, but I cannot find that he commits himself on the subject; certainly he cites no example from any cat of his own, and he offers scientific explanations. 'It is possible,' he concedes, 'that, even just for the briefest of moments, the vibration of sound in the air is accessible to the hyper-sensitivity of a cat.' But he also concedes that this does not explain the 'instinct for harmony, the taste for what is musically correct, that the composer Reynaldo Hahn assures us he has seen in cats'. The key word there, I think, is 'assures'; we have only the composer's word for it; which is not to suggest wilful deception, but only that a composer's cat might well become conditioned to certain sounds, react favourable to them, and unfavourably to others. I think, also, that people who love cats, or one particular cat, tend to see what they wish to see. Henri Sauguet, the composer, who always loved cats, was convinced that his cat Cody, whom he had had since childhood and who lived to a great age, shivered with ecstasy when he played the piano. Marcel Jouhandeau, who wrote a book about his cat, Minos, says that when he sings the cat comes and sniffs the song all round his mouth, tries to find it with his claws, 'and tries to make off with it', and that when he imitates a nightingale the cat becomes ecstatic.

I feel rather about such stories, given in good faith by intelligent people, as I do when people who believe in the survival of personality after physical death assure me they have actually seen someone they loved who had died. For them it is true; it could never be true for me.

In the matter of cats and their reaction to music I can only cite Lucy, who was obviously unpleasantly disturbed by it and tried to get away from it, and Sammy, who doesn't 'mind' it. When I first acquired a record-player I had it in the study, because I was writing a novel at that time in which I wanted to describe a boy singing like Maria Farandouri, and it helped me to listen to a record of her singing some songs of Theodorakis; when I first brought it into the room and opened it up and plugged it in Sammy, on the chair by my desk, watched with a good deal of curiosity; he is used to me sitting at this desk typing; he had never before seen me crouching over something on the floor and manipulating it; when I placed the record and pulled back the control which lowers it he jumped down from the chair and came over, fascinated by the drop of the record, the movement of the arm, the revolving of the disc. When the music began he watched for a little, then went and sat a little distance off and began to wash – indicating, I think, that enough was enough and that he really wasn't all that interested, and it was about time to be going out into the night anyhow.

When I next opened the record-player in his presence he was not interested, and when the music began ignored it. He looks up, usually, when it begins, if he is awake, listens for a moment then resumes whatever he was doing; when he is asleep or dozing the music appears not to impinge . . . whether it is Theodorakis or Johann Sebastian Bach, the only two composers I seem to play. Except, occasionally, the folk-singer, Julie Felix, and Sammy doesn't mind her either.

Michael Joseph – who lost count, he says, of the number of cats who at one time or another lived with him – writes in, *Cat's Company*, that his Siamese cat, Charles, was, like most of his cats, 'indifferent to radio and gramophone noises'. He does, however, record the case of a cat who was 'apparently a discriminating lover of music', in that he showed appreciation by purring and putting his paws on the singer's shoulder when 'She is Far From the Land' was sung in a beautiful tenor voice to a piano accompaniment, but who was left cold by other Irish songs and by all instrumental music. He adds, significantly, 'It appears to be more common, however, for animals to show signs of distress at vocal and instrumental music.'

Cats are said to detest whistling, the pitch being intolerable to them. Certainly my daughter once whistled in Mitzi's presence and the cat, to her shocked astonishment, flew at her. Remembering this I warned Catherine not to whistle when Sammy was around, she having newly acquired this art. 'Cats don't like whistling,' I said, and told her about Mitzi. This, of course, impelled her to whistle out of bravado, to see what Sammy would do. But he did nothing; he didn't mind. But then, as I have said, he doesn't mind music in general.

Since he ceased to be maladjusted he has become, really, a very amiable cat, this little tiger.

Chapter Fifteen

EXCEPT in the matter of dogs. Much as I admire and respect the late Michael Joseph as an authority on cats, I cannot agree with him that there is no endemic hostility between cats and dogs. Obviously a kitten and a puppy brought up together tolerate each other when they become mature cat and dog; my own view, based on observation, is that for the cat, at least, the dog is completely intolerable. I don't know enough about dogs to know whether the dog has this endemic aversion, but that it exists in the cat I am as sure as that it purrs.

Little feminine female Lucy would arch her back and become a hissing spitting fury at the sight of a dog pursuing his lawful business along the road, strictly minding his own leg-lifting business. The mere sight of a dog raises the hackles of any self-respecting cat – and cats are intensely self-respecting.

Recently I asked a neighbour if he would call in with Susie, the little Jack Russell bitch he had acquired, as I wanted a friend interested in these pretty little dogs to see it. When the little thing had been duly inspected and admired we all went out into the garden to admire the roses. I didn't know where Sammy was; as he wasn't in the house I supposed he was 'lying up' somewhere from the heat of the day. I have very often shown people round the garden during his siesta and he has never bothered to open even one eye. But then I have never shown people around with a *dog*. This little dog,

tripping along daintily in the wake of her master, brought
Sammy out of his nest under the azalea literally like a shot;
he shot out and stood on the low wall above the path, his
hackles up, hissing and spitting – at that pretty little inoffen-
sive female dog . . .

Susie recoiled in startled dismay; Sammy growled, and
Susie's owner, alarmed, picked her up.

'Oh dear!' he said.

Susie, however, did not feel oh dear at all, but strained
forward, eager to 'have at' the spiteful cat, and barking
angrily. The more Susie barked the more Sammy hissed,
growled, spat, and I began to feel oh dear myself.

'We'd better go,' my neighbour said, adding a little
bitterly, 'I'd forgotten you had a cat!'

I said, helplessly, apologetically, 'I didn't know he was
around . . . '

When the neighbour had gone, with Susie still held pro-
tectively in his arms, I went back to Sammy, who now sat
on the wall nonchalantly washing himself.

'There was no need to treat the poor little dog like that,'
I said.

He stopped washing and looked up at me and smiled – I
swear he smiled – blandly.

'That put the fear of cat into her,' he said.

'There was no need,' I repeated. 'She meant no harm.'

His green eyes, pale and cold, held mine for a moment,
contemptuously – then he went on washing. It is, really,
I suppose, the only way to deal with the illogicality of
human beings.

Later, when I was having tea on the loggia, he stalked
down the path and the steps and weaved about my legs.

'Go away,' I said. 'Beastly, horrible cat! I hate you!'

105

He went on weaving.

'Be reasonable,' he said. 'After all, I mean to say – a *dog* in the garden! Let's be friends. What about a catwich?'

'It's not crab today,' I said, harshly. 'Cucumber! Cats don't eat cucumber sandwiches! You're unlucky. Go away!'

But he didn't go away; instead, he clawed the sides of my chair, jumped up into my lap, then stood up on his hindlegs with his front paws on my chest and pushed his head against my face, purring loudly.

'Be *reasonable*!' he insisted. 'Be *nice*!'

Quite unreasonably I bent my head down to his and we pushed foreheads together.

'You're a horrible cat!' I said.

Quite often in our sixteen years together I shouted at Lucy that she was a hateful, horrible cat, and why didn't she get lost or drop dead – though, of course, if she had done either I should have been heartbroken. But a cat is not all sweetness and light; a cat can be damned irritating, getting under your feet when you're busy and expecting three people to lunch and everything hissing and steaming on the cooker and the table not yet laid, and pestering for food just because it can smell something cooking, and generally driving you crazy.

At first I never spoke crossly to Sammy, so anxious I was that he should settle down and be happy, terrified of undermining the sense of security I'd tried so hard to build up in him. Now that he does feel himself secure he comes in for his share of harsh words. Very often when I am cooking and he is plaguing me with lies about being starving I swoop down on him in a rage and dump him in another room.

The food-consciousness of the domestic cat is past belief.

A cat will only recently have had a good meal but still fancy a taste of what humans are eating. Sammy loves fish, both cooked and raw, liver cooked or raw, but preferably raw, raw minced beef, and though he will eat all the tinned cat foods there is only one of which he will eat a tin in one go; but his favourite food, far and away, is chicken – which dates from his Ilford days, though there I have an idea he didn't get much if anything more than the skin, for there were after all three children in the family. I never give him the skin; I may be wrong, but I somehow think it is not good for a cat, being so greasy, and, I would think, indigestible. What he gets from me when I roast a chicken is a heaped saucerful of small pieces prised from the carcase and the neck after the bird has been carved for the guests. He doesn't get the liver, because though the first meal he ever had with me was chicken's liver, specially bought for him, when I roast a chicken I consider the liver a *bonne bouche* for anyone who can appreciate it, and I am always sorry that a chicken hasn't *two* livers . . .

But Sammy gets his helping of chicken, and never, ever, is he given bones. It is an article of faith with me that when you feed a cat chicken scraps, or cooked rabbit, or fish, it should all be gone-through with the fingers, to feel for bones. I am prepared to believe that *uncooked* chicken or rabbit bones are all right, but somehow I have never felt able to risk it . . . not being absolutely convinced; or, perhaps, unable to overcome a prejudice.

When I give Sammy the chicken he so enormously relishes I find myself recalling the 'pigeon restaurants' along the Nile in Cairo, and the swarms of homeless, starving cats who gather there, and to whom the diners throw the skin and bones of the grilled pigeons which constitute the only dish served by these restaurants. At the time I never thought about it, but I have since wondered how many of these wretched cats get bones lodged in their gullets, or, worse still, in their intestines.

These open-air, riverside restaurants, with their tables ranged beside the parapet, and lights strung in the tall eucalyptus trees, are very pleasant, especially when the Nile is in flood and only a foot below the parapet. The Egyptian night is always beautiful, whether it is in its winter and spring warmth, or its welcome summer and autumn coolness – or relative coolness. The Egyptian beer is good, also the wines from the Gianaclis vineyards at Alexandria; and the pigeons are done to a turn . . . but the pleasure of dining in such places is spoilt by the miserable cats. The Egyptians shoo them away, impatiently; it takes a 'sentimental' Englishwoman to be upset about them. When you fling a morsel to them half a dozen of the gaunt creatures swoop on it and fight savagely for it; then you try to get something to a wretched cat who seems to be not good at fending for itself, and your Egyptian host becomes irritated, declaring that you are feeding most of your dinner to the cats . . . which is true. After a time I would not go to these pigeon restaurants, much as I liked the setting and the food. But there is a pestering of starving cats at all open-air restaurants in Cairo, though the pigeon restaurants are the most afflicted.

Sammy, you do not know how lucky you are, I think when I set a piled-up saucer of boneless, skinless chicken scraps before him. Yet, I suppose, if he were a Cairo cat, born into homelessness and starvation, he would cope; he would survive – emaciated, and with cauliflower ears, and one eye, perhaps, like some of the battle-scarred toms, but with enough life in him to fight for scraps of food and for females, enough vitality on his starvation diet to procreate – unfortunately. Ripeness is all, I know, but not in Cairo; there 'twere better both for human beings and for animals that the slogan should be 'let sterilization thrive!' In Ancient Egypt, as we know, the cat was venerated, but that is millennia ago. Perhaps even today an Egyptian would not harm a cat – whilst not being disturbed by its hunger and homelessness. Like the Burmese Buddhists who will not have unwanted kittens and puppies destroyed, but take them to deserted graveyards and dump them among the ancient tombstones, to survive as best they can; they die of starvation, of course, being too young to fend for themselves, but those who have dumped them have not destroyed life. Oh, no.

Which is a long way from Sammy and his passion for chicken, but sometimes one is seized by what Blake liked to call a 'righteous indignation'. To get as far away from humbug as possible it is pleasant to recall that Dr Johnson fed his famous cat, Hodge, on oysters, which must have been lovely for Hodge, and galling for that cat-disliking and generally unlikeable literary leech, Boswell. In those days, no doubt, oysters were not the luxury they are now; Johnson was hardly a man of means. He had other cats he liked better than Hodge, he declared, but it is Hodge, that 'very fine cat', who has achieved fame.

Throughout history, it seems, most writers have liked cats, preferring them to dogs. It is understandable; a cat is a quiet creature; is not obtrusive. Théophile Gautier, who had a passion for cats, writing of Baudelaire's poems to cats as 'mystic masterpieces', said that cats 'like silence, order and quietness, and no place is so proper for them as the study of a man of letters'. I think myself that Gautier grossly overdid it when writing about cats and their communion with writers' thoughts, and so forth, but that they appeal to writers because of their quietness, their withdrawn quality, is undoubtedly true.

There is also the aesthetic appeal; they are surely of all creatures the most beautiful, the most graceful, the most aesthetically satisfying. I seldom look at this Sammy-cat without thinking how beautiful he is – the wonderful colouring and markings of his coat, the honey colour blending into dark amber, the bold patterning, and added to all this the combination of grace and dignity in his movements. Sometimes he seems such a strong, proud, arrogant little animal; at other times, when he snuggles up against me at breakfast time, like a child, resting a paw on the hand nearest him, he seems so small, almost feminine; and at yet other times, when he pitches down head first on to a rug and rolls over, paws raised, soft furry belly exposed, inviting play, kittenish; but always, in all his aspects, beautiful.

I do not think he is the 'most beautiful cat in the world'; I am well aware that there are very many more beautiful cats – elegant, exquisitely coloured Siamese, the 'prince of cats', sleek, seal-like Abyssinians and Russian Blues, Silver Tabbies with marvellous dark markings, all manner of beautiful cats, thoroughbred, flawless. Almost all cats are beautiful, but obviously some are more beautiful than others. This Sammy-cat, this little sturdy Ilford tiger, is a long way from being flawless, with his black-freckled nose and mouth, and his serrated ears, damaged in battles long ago, but he is all the same beautiful, and what Dr Johnson said of his Hodge, 'a fine cat, a very fine cat indeed'.

It is nearly four years ago, now, as I write this, that he

was brought here in the beastly basket from the vet's, yelling his head off, 'Help! help!', but so much part of the scene, and of my life, has he become that it seems much longer. He has settled down as though he has never lived anywhere else. We get along; we understand each other, after a fashion – imperfectly, but well enough. Night after night I sit here, burning the midnight electricity, whilst he is somewhere out there in the midnight darkness or the midnight moonlight, being his nocturnal cat self.

This is not the end of the story; it cannot be, since he is still only about half way through his allotted span, but it is the most important part – the story of his rehabilitation in a new life, of his escape from the-fate-worse-than-death, and his survival of the great ill that befell him. The rest could only be a repetitious narrative of his wanderings in the night – and fictitious at that, since I do not know where he goes or what he does, and he cannot tell me, and I have no means of finding out.

It is anyhow none of my business.